THE
SPIRIT

Witness Lee

Living Stream Ministry
Anaheim, CA • www.lsm.org

First Edition, November 1990.

ISBN 978-0-87083-553-7

Published by

Living Stream Ministry
2431 W. La Palma Ave., Anaheim, CA 92801 U.S.A.
P. O. Box 2121, Anaheim, CA 92814 U.S.A.

Printed in the United States of America

10 11 12 13 14 15 16 / 11 10 9 8 7 6 5 4

CONTENTS

PREFACE

This book is composed of messages given by Brother Witness Lee from February through June of 1990 in a full-time training in Anaheim, California.

CHAPTER ONE

THE DIFFERENT ASPECTS OF THE SPIRIT

(1)

Scripture Reading: John 4:24; Gen. 1:2; Rom. 8:9; 1 Cor. 2:11; Matt. 28:19; 2 Cor. 13:14; Judg. 6:34; Isa. 61:1; Luke 4:18; Acts 5:9; 8:39; 2 Cor. 3:17; Luke 1:35; Matt. 1:18,20; Luke 4:1; Matt. 3:16; Acts 10:38; Matt. 12:28

We need to enter into the significance of all the different aspects of the Spirit. We need a vision of all these different aspects which will give us a clear view of the Spirit. Once we see something, we will never forget it. In 1958 I came to the United States, and someone took me to see Disneyland. I could never forget Disneyland because I saw it. I received a "vision" of Disneyland, and what I saw was impressed into my being. In like manner, we need to see visions concerning the Spirit. This series of messages is entitled *The Spirit*. "The Spirit" is the simplest divine title of the Spirit of God in the Bible. What I will share in these messages is the accumulation of all the visions which I have seen through my study of the Bible over many years.

Basically speaking, what is revealed in the Bible is God. We have to realize that the center of the Bible is God. Of course, God is embodied in Christ. God is the source, Christ is the embodiment of the source, and this Christ is realized as the Spirit. The Spirit is the reaching of God to us and the realization of the embodiment of God. God is embodied in Christ, and Christ is realized as the Spirit. Thus, the Spirit is the realization of Christ, and Christ is the embodiment of the very God who is the source of everything.

In the first verse of the Bible, there is God—"In the

beginning God created the heavens and the earth" (Gen. 1:1—ASV). The second verse of the Bible tells us that the Spirit of God brooded over the face of the waters. Thus, the first two verses of the Bible speak of God and of the Spirit of God. In the first chapter of the Bible, there is not the term *Christ,* the Messiah, the Anointed One, but there are a number of things typifying Christ. In chapters one and two of Genesis, four items typify Christ: the light, the sun, the man Adam as the head over all things, and the tree of life. Although the title *Christ,* the Messiah, the Anointed One, is not mentioned, the very person of Christ is typified as the light, as the sun, as the head of God's creation, and as the tree of life. Therefore, the Triune God is in the first two chapters of the Bible. In these first two chapters are God, the Spirit, and four types of Christ. Now we want to go on to see the different aspects of the Spirit of the Triune God.

SPIRIT—THE ESSENCE OF GOD

Spirit is the essence of God. John 4:24 says, "God is Spirit." This verse does not say that God is "the" Spirit but that God is Spirit. To insert a definite article, "the," in this verse is wrong. John 4:24 does not show us "the" Spirit. It only says, "God is Spirit." This is just like saying that a table is wood. We would not say that a table is "the" wood. That is wrong. When we say that a table is wood, this indicates that the essence of the table is wood. To say that a ring on a person's finger is gold means that the ring's essence is gold. John 4:24 shows us what God's essence is. God's essence is Spirit. In order to touch God and experience God, we need to know what His essence is.

Now we need to see the distinction among four words: nature, substance, essence, and element. In the theological study of the Trinity, these four words have been used. An element is a substance. Every element has its nature, and in the nature of the element is the essence. Consequently, the essence denotes the very thing itself. Now we can see that there is a difference in using the two words *essence* and *substance.* We cannot refer to the substance of the essence but to the essence of the substance. Each substance or substantial element has its essence. God is Spirit, and Spirit is the essence of God.

THE SPIRIT OF GOD, THE HOLY SPIRIT— THE THIRD IN THE PERSON OF THE TRIUNE GOD

The Spirit is the Spirit of God, the Holy Spirit—the third in the person of the Triune God (Gen. 1:2; Rom. 8:9; 1 Cor. 2:11; Matt. 28:19; 2 Cor. 13:14). In the Bible the Spirit of God is first mentioned as the brooding Spirit. Genesis 1:2 says that the Spirit of God was brooding upon the face of the waters. The brooding of a hen over its eggs is for the purpose of producing some living things. The Spirit of God was brooding, stretching out His wings, over the death situation for the purpose of producing life. The Spirit of God in Genesis 1:2 is for God's move in His creation.

In the New Testament, the Spirit of God is mainly mentioned for God's new creation. In God's old creation, the Spirit of God brooded. In God's new creation, the Spirit of God does not just brood over us, but He has entered into us and dwells in us. This is mentioned in Romans 8. In the Old Testament, the Spirit of God moved to brood over the face of the waters for the producing of life in God's old creation. In the New Testament, the Spirit of God also moves and acts in God's new creation, but He does this in a deeper and a more subjective way. In the New Testament, the Spirit of God dwells in us.

First Corinthians 2:11b-12 says, "So also the things of God no one has known except the Spirit of God. Now we have received not the spirit of the world, but the Spirit which is from God, that we may know the things which have been freely given to us by God." This means that the moving Spirit of God is also the revealing Spirit. When He moves in us, that is, when He dwells in us, He reveals to us the things of God. This very Spirit—the moving One, the indwelling One, the revealing One—is the third in the divine Person. The third means the ultimate one, the last one. Matthew 28:19 gives us the complete title of the divine Trinity—the Father, the Son, and the Holy Spirit. Our God is one God, but our one God has three aspects. He is one but in three persons.

Verse 1 of hymn #608 in *Hymns,* says:

> What mystery, the Father, Son, and Spirit,
> In person three, in substance all are one.
> How glorious, this God our being enters
> To be our all, thru Spirit in the Son!

Instead of saying, "In person three, in substance all are one," it would be better to say, "In substance three, in essence all are one." We may say that God has three substances, but only one essence. In the three substances of the divine Trinity, the Holy Spirit, or the Spirit of God, is the third one. He is the consummated One, and this consummated One is the consummation of the Triune God. When the Triune God was consummated, He was revealed in the way that we who believe into Christ can be baptized into Him. This indicates that we, the believers of Christ, can have an organic union with the consummated Triune God.

The first time that the New Testament speaks of our spiritual baptism, it says that we are baptized into the name of the Father, the Son, and the Holy Spirit. Later, when the Acts and the Epistles speak concerning spiritual baptism, they speak of being baptized in the Spirit (Acts 1:5; 1 Cor. 12:13). This indicates that when we are baptized into the Spirit, we are baptized into the Triune God—the Father, the Son, and the Spirit. This is because the Spirit is the consummation and the totality of the Triune God. The Father as the source is embodied in the Son, and the Son as the embodiment of the Father is realized as the Spirit. Therefore, all three of the Triune God are present in the Spirit. When we were baptize in the Spirit, or into the Spirit, we were baptized into the Triune God. The Spirit has become the consummation of the Triune God.

When this consummation had been accomplished, the Triune God was ready for us to get into Him, to have an organic union with Him. Before the consummation of the Spirit, the Triune God was not ready for anyone to get into Him. Thus, baptism was not in the Old Testament. Baptism into the Triune God was only begun after the accomplishment of Christ's resurrection. His resurrection was the final step for the Triune God to be processed and to be consummated. After that step the Spirit had been consummated, which means that the Triune God had been consummated. The consummated Spirit is the consummation of the Triune God. After this consummation, the Triune God was ready for us to be organically united with Him.

Because we are now in the Triune God, 2 Corinthians 13:14 tells us that the grace of the Son, the love of the Father, and the fellowship of the Spirit is with us for our portion, for our enjoyment. Matthew 28:19 shows the organic union we have with the Triune God because we have been baptized into Him. Second Corinthians 13:14 shows us that in this organic union we have a fellowship. This fellowship is the flow of the consummated Spirit in the source of God's love and in the passage of the Son's grace.

The Bible shows us first that the Spirit of God moved in God's old creation. Second, the same moving Spirit in God's new creation dwells in us to reveal all the things of God to us. This Spirit—the moving Spirit, the indwelling Spirit, the revealing Spirit—has been consummated to be the third in the divine person of the processed and consummated Triune God. Now the Triune God is ready for His chosen people to get into Him, to have an organic union with Him, making them one with Him. Day after day we can enjoy Him as our portion from the Father's love, through the Son's grace, and by the fellowship, the flow, of the Spirit.

THE SPIRIT OF JEHOVAH,
THE SPIRIT OF THE LORD—THE REACHING OF GOD

The Spirit of Jehovah, the Spirit of the Lord, is the reaching of God (Judg. 6:34; Isa. 61:1; Luke 4:18; Acts 5:9; 8:39; 2 Cor. 3:17). "The Spirit of Jehovah" in the Old Testament is "the Spirit of the Lord" in the New Testament. This is proven by comparing Isaiah 61:1 with Luke 4:18. Isaiah 61:1 says, "The Spirit of the Lord Jehovah is upon me" (ASV). When this verse is quoted in Luke 4:18, it says, "The Spirit of the Lord is upon Me." These two verses show that the Spirit of the Lord in the New Testament is the same as the Spirit of Jehovah in the Old Testament.

The Spirit of the Lord, or the Spirit of Jehovah, is the reaching of God to us. When God comes to us, that means He reaches us. In His reaching, He is called the Spirit of Jehovah, the Spirit of the Lord. Two verses in the book of Acts confirm this. In Acts 5:9, Peter said to Sapphira, "Why was it agreed together by you to test the Spirit of the Lord?" Peter's word to Sapphira indicates that the Spirit of the Lord is in the church. His presence, His reaching. His coming, is in the church. He is not far away. This was Peter's thought. It was as if he were saying, "Don't you realize that the Spirit is here? I have the reaching, the presence, of the Spirit of the Lord. When you deceive me, you deceive Him." Acts 8:39 tells us that "the Spirit of the Lord caught away Philip." The Spirit of the Lord reached Philip and took him away. Second Corinthians 3:17 says that the Lord is the Spirit and where the Spirit of the Lord is, there is liberty. "Where the Spirit of the Lord is," is the reaching of the Spirit.

THE ESSENTIAL SPIRIT—
OF WHOM JESUS WAS BORN
AND WITH WHOM JESUS WAS FILLED

The New Testament reveals that Jesus was born of the essential Spirit and filled with the essential Spirit. Luke 1 and Matthew 1 unveil to us that Jesus was born of the Spirit. The Spirit was the very essence of the person of Jesus. Therefore, this Spirit is the essential Spirit. From the birth of Jesus, this essential Spirit never left Him. Actually, the essential Spirit could not leave Him because this Spirit was His essence. The essence is the very intrinsic matter of a substance. A piece of wood, for example, is a substance, and in this substance there is an essence. The essence could never leave this substance. We may say that Jesus is the substance. Within Jesus is His essence, and this essence is the essential Spirit. He was born of the essential Spirit, and He was also filled with this essential Spirit.

THE ECONOMICAL SPIRIT—
IN WHOM JESUS WAS BAPTIZED AND EMPOWERED

Jesus was born of the essential Spirit and filled with the

essential Spirit. Then when He came out to start His ministry at the age of thirty, He needed another aspect of the Spirit. This was the economical aspect of power for the work. The essential aspect of the Spirit is for the intrinsic nature within. The economical aspect of the Spirit is for the power without. He needed both aspects for His living and for His ministry.

Jesus was born of the essential Spirit and filled with the essential Spirit, but when He went out to minister. He needed the power. Thus, when He came out of the water of baptism, the Spirit as the economical Spirit descended upon Him (Matt. 3:16). According to Luke 4:18, He was anointed by God with this economical, descending Spirit. Within, Jesus was constituted and filled with the essential Spirit. Without, Jesus was anointed and empowered with the economical Spirit. Therefore, He was a person wrapped up with the Spirit. The Spirit within Him was essential, and the Spirit outside of Him was economical. The essential Spirit is for life and nature, and the economical Spirit is for power to do the work. Jesus was wrapped up with the Spirit of God in these two aspects.

Today we need the same two aspects of the Spirit of God. The Spirit of God is God reaching us to be life and nature to us and also to be power to us. We must be filled with the essential Spirit and anointed with the economical Spirit.

QUESTIONS AND ANSWERS

Question: I do not understand how the Triune God is three in substance and one in essence. Could you speak more concerning this?

Answer: We may use a table with four legs to illustrate this matter. We can say that the four legs of the table are the four substances. Each piece is a substance. The table, however, has only one essence. In the same way, the Father, the Son, and the Spirit are three substances, but the Triune God has only one essence.

Question: I have a question concerning note 3 in 1 John 1:5 of the Recovery Version. This note says, "In His nature God is Spirit, love, and light. Spirit denotes the nature of God's Person; love, the nature of God's essence; and light, the nature of God's expression." This note says that Spirit denotes the nature of God's Person, while John 4:24 reveals that Spirit is the essence of God. Can you share more concerning this?

Answer: God being Spirit refers to His person. God being love refers to His intrinsic essence. God being light refers to His expression. In the person is the essence, and outside of the person is the expression. God's being is Spirit; God's essence is love; and God's expression is light. From within, God is love. From without, God is light.

Spirit is the nature of God's person and also the essence of the nature. God is a person, a being. This person, this living being, has a nature. That nature is Spirit. In the person is the nature, and in the nature is the essence. The person, the nature, and the essence are all the Spirit. The divine essence has different aspects. The essence of God is not only Spirit but also love. Actually, the Spirit of God is the love of God.

The Spirit is the person of God, the nature of God, and the essence of God. If you call on the name of Jesus, you get His person. His person is the Spirit. The Spirit is not only the person of God but also the person of Christ. This Spirit is also the nature of God and the essence of God. That means that the Spirit is God. God is Spirit, God is love, and God is light. Light is God's expression, expressing God as love, and this love is just the Spirit. Eventually, God, love, light, the Spirit, and Jesus Christ are all one. This is our wonderful God!

Question: Are the economical Spirit and the essential Spirit the same Spirit?

Answer: The economical Spirit and the essential Spirit are two aspects of the same Spirit. The same Spirit has two kinds of functions. Inwardly for our life and living, the Spirit is essential. Outwardly for our ministry and work, the same Spirit is economical. Jesus had the Spirit essentially from His birth. Suddenly, when He came out of the water of baptism, the Spirit descended upon Him. This is not another Spirit, but the same Spirit in the economical sense. The Bible tells us that Christ was born of the Spirit. He was full of the Spirit all the time. But still the Spirit descended upon Him. The Spirit was with Him already essentially, but in the sense of economy for God's administration, God's arrangement, the

Spirit was not with Him. Economically speaking, the Spirit came upon Jesus when He was baptized. These are not two Spirits, but the same Spirit in two aspects.

When a brother exercises his spirit to deal with his wife by the Spirit and not by himself, he is enjoying the essential aspect of the Spirit. When a brother exercises his spirit to minister the Word by the Spirit and not by himself, he is experiencing both the essential and the economical aspects of the Spirit. Because the experience of the Spirit is altogether abstract and mysterious, we need to exercise our faith. In Ephesians 3 Paul asked the Father to grant us to be strengthened with power through His Spirit into the inner man, that Christ might make His home in our hearts through faith (vv. 16-17). We should not neglect this small phrase— "through faith." We have to believe. If we say that we do not feel that Christ is in us, we have annulled this fact by our unbelief. Instead we should say, "Praise the Lord! Christ is in me." In spite of not having any feeling, we can still exercise our spirit of faith to declare that Christ is in us. When we do this, we confirm this fact by faith.

We need to experience the Spirit by faith. When we go out to preach the gospel, we should not say that we do not feel that we have the economical Spirit. Sometimes we may not even feel that we have the essential Spirit. The more we pay attention to our feelings, the more we lose everything positive. Instead we should pray, "Lord, thank You that I am saved. Thank You that You are in me and that I am in You. Thank You that I am abiding in You and that You are abiding in me." The more we speak this way, the more we confirm the divine facts by faith. We may even shout, "Hallelujah! The Lord dwells in me! Hallelujah! I have the power of the economical Spirit!" When we declare the facts in this way, the facts become ours. I admire Paul's writing in Ephesians 3— "That Christ may make His home in your hearts through faith" (v. 17). If the two words "through faith" are deleted, everything positive is gone. Our experience of Christ is altogether a matter of the Spirit through faith.

CHAPTER TWO

THE DIFFERENT ASPECTS OF THE SPIRIT

(2)

Scripture Reading: 1 Cor. 15:45; Rom. 8:2; John 14:16-17; 15:26; 16:13; 1 John 5:6; Acts 16:7; Rom. 8:9; Phil. 1:19; 2 Cor. 3:17-18; Exo. 30:22-31; 1 John 2:20, 27; 2 Cor. 1:21; Rom. 8:4-6, 16; 1 Cor. 6:17; Rev. 1:4; 4:5; 5:6; Exo. 25:31, 37; Zech. 4:2, 10; 3:9; John 7:39; 1 Pet. 1:2; Rev. 22:17a

In the previous message, we saw five aspects of the Spirit. In this message we want to go further to see eleven more aspects. Whenever we speak concerning the Spirit, this involves the study of the divine Trinity. In studying the divine Trinity, I would recommend chapters seven and eight of *Elders' Training—Book 3, The Way to Carry Out the Vision.* There are two main points in the study of the divine Trinity. One point refers to the one God, and the other point refers to the Three of the Godhead. The word *triune* means three-one. On the one hand, God is one yet three. On the other hand, God is three yet one. We may say that God is three in person but one in essence.

In the last message, we talked about the words *element, substance, nature,* and *essence.* Another word used in relation to the Trinity is *hypostasis.* This anglicized Greek word is actually composed of two Greek words—*hupo* meaning under or below and stasis meaning substantial support. This word refers to the three substances of the divine Trinity. The Father, the Son, and the Spirit are the three hypostases, or substances, of the divine Trinity.

A Latin word used to equal *hypostasis* in the theological

study of the Trinity was the word *persona*. *Persona* is where we get the English word *person*. In the study of the divine Trinity, Bible teachers say that God is three persons in one essence. Regarding the Three of the Triune God, theologians have used the Greek word *hypostasis,* the Latin word *persona,* and the English word *person*. These words refer to God being three.

The Triune God is also one in essence. The Greek word *ousia* refers to the essence of the substance. A table made of wood has wood as its substance, and within this substance is the essence. The Latin word for essence is *essentia*. The Triune God is three *hypostases* in one *ousia*. In other words. God is three persons in one essence. The persons should not be confused, and the essence should not be divided. The Three are one in essence. This is why we can say that when the Son comes, the Father comes, and when the Son and the Father are here, the Spirit is also here. Since one is here, all of the Three are here because in essence, They are one.

We have to be careful, however, when we use the word *person* to describe the Three of the Godhead. W. Griffith Thomas, the founder of Dallas Theological Seminary, indicated that we may borrow a word like *person* to define the Trinity because our human language is inadequate, but if we press the term *person* too far, it will lead to tritheism. It is safer to say that God has three substances but only one essence. I hope that this discussion of these terms will help us in our understanding of the divine Trinity. Now we want to fellowship concerning more aspects of the Spirit.

THE LIFE-GIVING SPIRIT— CHRIST BECOMING THE LIFE-GIVING SPIRIT IN HIS RESURRECTION

According to 1 Corinthians 15:45 the Spirit is the life-giving Spirit, and Christ became this life-giving Spirit in His resurrection. The life-giving Spirit has the ability to give us life. The Spirit is moving, working, and living in us to impart life into us. The life-giving Spirit is now working and moving in the being of the believers. The Spirit is the life-imparting Spirit, working to give life to our whole being.

THE SPIRIT OF LIFE—
THE PNEUMATIC CHRIST IN RESURRECTION
BEING THE SPIRIT OF THE DIVINE LIFE
TO HIS BELIEVERS

The Spirit of life is the pneumatic Christ in resurrection as the Spirit of the divine life to His believers. The term *the Spirit of life* is used only once in the New Testament—in Romans 8:2. The Spirit is not only the life-giving Spirit but also the Spirit of life. The Spirit of life is the reality of life, for this Spirit contains the element of the divine life. Actually, the Spirit Himself is life. Therefore, with the Spirit of life, we have the riches of the divine life.

THE SPIRIT OF REALITY—
THE SPIRIT OF WHAT GOD IS, HAS, AND DOES

In John 14:6 the Lord Jesus said that He was the way, the reality, and the life. This shows us that life and reality are related. Reality is life and life is reality. The reality of our person, of our being, is our human life. Likewise, the reality of God is the divine life. The Spirit of life is the Spirit of reality.

The Spirit of reality is the Spirit of what God is, has, and does. In other words, the Spirit of reality is the Spirit of God's being, of God's possession, and of God's doing. In John 14:16 and 17, the Lord said, "And I will ask the Father, and He will give you another Comforter, that He may be with you forever; even the Spirit of reality, whom the world cannot receive, because it does not behold Him or know Him; but you know Him, because He abides with you and shall be in you." When the Lord referred to "another Comforter," He was saying that this Comforter was Himself in another form. He was a Comforter in the flesh, but in resurrection He became the Spirit, which would be another Comforter. This Spirit is the Spirit of reality, who is the reality of Christ. He is the real Christ, the real Jesus.

John 15:26 and 16:13 also refer to the Spirit of reality. In John 16:13, the Lord Jesus said that the Spirit of reality would guide us into all the reality. In 16:15 He said, "All that the Father has is Mine; therefore I said that He receives of

Mine and shall disclose it to you." All that the Father is and
has is the Son's, and all that the Son is and has is received by
the Spirit. Then the Spirit discloses all of this to us to be our
portion. The Spirit of reality makes everything of the Triune
God ours.

In the sense of worship, God is three-in-one. But in the
actual, daily life experience of the believer who is enjoying
the Lord, the three-in-one God is one with the believers. The
Father, the Son, and the Spirit are three-in-one, and They
are one with the believers, including you and me. This is
because we are in Christ, the embodiment of the Triune God,
and He is in us. In our worship, we worship the three-in-one
God. We worship the Father, the Son, and the Spirit as one
God. We worship our God, who is three-in-one. But in our
Christian experience, the three-in-one God is one with us.
This is because we are one with the Father, one with the Son,
and one with the Spirit. We are all one in the Triune God in
one essence. All of us are in the same divine essence because
we all have received the divine nature. Second Peter 1:4 says
that we have all been made partakers of the divine nature.
Within the divine nature is the divine essence. As we have
seen, essence is more intrinsic than nature.

We are one with the Triune God because the Spirit of real-
ity makes God real to us. In whatever Christ is, in whatever
He has, and in whatever He has done, He is one with us.
Therefore, His experiences have become our history. We were
crucified with Him (Gal. 2:20). His crucifixion is our history.
We have also been resurrected with Him (Eph. 2:6). Whatever
He is, is ours; whatever He has, is ours; and whatever He has
done, is ours. We have passed through all the processes which
our Triune God has passed through because we are in Him.
Even humanly speaking, we may say that the experiences of
our fore fathers are our history. When a person's great-grand-
father came to the United States, that person came with him
and in him. Hebrews 7 tells us that when Abraham paid
tithes to Melchisedec, Levi also paid them because he was in
the loins of his father when Melchisedec met him (vv. 9-10).
Levi, as a great-grandson of Abraham, offered something to
Melchisedec before he was born because he was in Abraham.

We can also say that before we were born, we were crucified, buried, and resurrected with Christ through the Spirit. Without the Spirit, there is no linking between us and the Triune God. The Spirit of reality is the linking between us and the Triune God, making us one with the Triune God in experience.

THE SPIRIT OF JESUS—
THE SPIRIT OF JESUS IN HIS SUFFERING HUMANITY

Acts 16:7 says, "When they had come down to Mysia, they tried to go into Bithynia, and the Spirit of Jesus did not allow them." The Spirit of Jesus is a particular expression concerning the Spirit of God and refers to the Spirit of the incarnated Savior who, as Jesus in His humanity, passed through human living and death on the cross. This indicates that in the Spirit of Jesus there is not only the divine element of God but also the human element and the elements of His human living and His suffering of death. Such an all-inclusive Spirit was needed by Paul in his preaching ministry, a ministry of suffering among human beings and for human beings in the human life. The Spirit of Jesus is the reality of Jesus in His suffering humanity. If we do not have this Spirit of Jesus, Jesus will not be real to us. But today Jesus is real to us because we have the Spirit of Jesus as the reality, the realization, of Jesus.

THE SPIRIT OF CHRIST—
THE SPIRIT OF CHRIST IN HIS RESURRECTED LIFE

In Romans 8:9 Paul speaks of the Spirit of Christ. The emphasis of the Spirit of Jesus is upon humanity and the capacity for suffering. But the emphasis of the Spirit of Christ is upon the resurrection and the imparting of life. The Spirit of Christ is the Spirit of the resurrected and life-giving Christ. By the Spirit of Christ we can partake of the power of His resurrection, identified with Him in the transcendency of His ascension and in the authority of His enthronement. By the Spirit of Christ we partake of His resurrection life, His resurrection power, His transcendency, and His reigning authority.

THE SPIRIT OF JESUS CHRIST—
THE SPIRIT OF THE SUFFERING JESUS
AND THE RESURRECTED CHRIST

Philippians 1:19 speaks of the bountiful supply of the Spirit of Jesus Christ. Because the Spirit of Jesus has particular reference to the Lord's suffering, and the Spirit of Christ to His resurrection, the Spirit of Jesus Christ is related to both suffering and resurrection. The Spirit of Jesus Christ is the Spirit of the Jesus who lived a life of suffering on earth and of the Christ who is now in resurrection. In his suffering Paul experienced both the Lord's suffering in His humanity and the Lord's resurrection. Hence, to Paul the Spirit was the Spirit of Jesus Christ, the compound, all-inclusive, life-giving Spirit of the Triune God. Such a Spirit has and even is the bountiful supply for a person like Paul who was experiencing and enjoying Christ in His human living and resurrection.

THE LORD SPIRIT—THE LORD WHO IS THE SPIRIT,
AND THE SPIRIT WHO IS THE LORD

The Lord Spirit is the Lord who is the Spirit and the Spirit who is the Lord (2 Cor. 3:17-18). Second Corinthians 3:18 speaks of the Lord Spirit. According to the context of 2 Corinthians 3, the Lord is Jehovah God. According to the New Testament, Jehovah God is altogether embodied in Jesus Christ. In Matthew 1 the Lord Jesus was given two names. Jesus was His God-given name, and Emmanuel was the name called by man. Jesus means Jehovah the Savior. Emmanuel means God with us. "Je" in the name Jesus is the short form of Jehovah. "El" in the name Emmanuel means God in Hebrew. Therefore, in the two names given to the Lord, there are Jehovah and God. In Jesus is Jehovah, and in Emmanuel is God. Thus, Jesus is Jehovah God. This Jehovah God is the Lord both in the Old Testament and in the New Testament.

Second Corinthians 3 unveils how this Lord, who is the embodiment of Jehovah God, is now the Spirit. Therefore, He has a compound title—"the Lord Spirit." The Lord Spirit may be considered a compound title like the Father God and the Lord Christ. This title signifies that Jehovah God, who is the Lord, is now the Spirit. We are being transformed into Christ's image from glory to glory as from the Lord Spirit.

The Lord Spirit is for our transformation. Whenever we call, "O Lord," we get the Spirit. We can be transformed by calling "O Lord" again and again throughout the day. When we call "O Lord," the Spirit comes. In the whole universe, there is only one Lord. Among all the founders of great religions, not one is called the Lord. The only one who is called the Lord is Jesus. When we call "O Lord," we get the Spirit, the Lord Spirit. This Spirit is the transforming Spirit. The way to deal with our temper is to call, "O Lord Spirit." If we are quick persons, how can we have a change? We need to call, "O Lord Spirit." If a quick person called, "O Lord Spirit" again and again for two weeks, he would be slowed down. The Lord Spirit changes us, transforms us. He transforms us into the image of the resurrected and glorified Christ from glory to glory.

THE COMPOUNDED SPIRIT—THE COMPOUND SPIRIT TYPIFIED BY THE COMPOUND OINTMENT

The compounded Spirit is the compound Spirit typified by the compound ointment (Exo. 30:22-31). An ointment is composed of some elements compounded with oil. In the old edition of the Newberry Bible, there is a note in Exodus 30 that says the anointing oil refers to the Holy Spirit. The Newberry Bible was put out by the open Brethren. The Lord went on to show us that the Spirit, typified by the ointment, is a compound Spirit. The Brethren saw that the anointing ointment in Exodus 30 is the Holy Spirit, but they did not see that this Holy Spirit, as typified in Exodus 30, is a compound Spirit. This Spirit is compounded with a number of elements.

Man and God Compounded Together

The compound ointment is composed first of a hin of olive oil. Then four spices are added to the oil. These spices, or elements, are myrrh, cinnamon, calamus, and cassia. When these four elements are blended with the oil, they become a compound ointment. The one hin of olive oil is compounded with four elements. The number one refers to the unique God, and the number four refers to the creatures. Among the creatures, man takes the lead, so we can say that the number four refers to man. Man is typified by the four spices of the plant life. The compounding of the four spices with the oil signifies that man and God are compounded together.

Flowing Myrrh—the Sweet Death of Christ

Flowing myrrh refers to the sweet death of Christ. His death is a positive death. The only death in the whole universe that is positive is Christ's death. The death of Christ is sweet.

Sweet Cinnamon—the Sweet Effectiveness of Christ's Death

Sweet cinnamon typifies the sweet effectiveness of Christ's death. The positive death of Christ signified by myrrh is very fragrant, full of cinnamon. Cinnamon adds flavor and sweetness to food. If we are not experiencing Christ's death, our life is not very sweet. When a husband and wife quarrel, that is not sweet. How can they neutralize such a situation? They need to put the death of Christ into their marriage life. Then their marriage life will be sweet. If a person does not have the cross in his daily life, it will be hard to get along with him. The sweet death of Christ needs to be added to our daily life.

Sweet Calamus— the Power of Christ's Resurrection

The third element added to the oil is sweet calamus, which signifies the power of Christ's resurrection. Calamus is a reed that grows in a marsh or a muddy place. Even though it grows in a marsh, it is able to shoot up into the air. According to the sequence of the spices, calamus signifies the rising up of the Lord Jesus from the place of death. The Lord was put into a marsh, into a death situation, but in resurrection He rose up and stood up.

Cassia—the Flavor of the Power of Christ's Resurrection

Cassia signifies the flavor of the power of Christ's resurrection. In ancient times, cassia was a repellent to insects and snakes. Only the power of the resurrected Christ can repel all the evil "insects" and especially the old serpent, the devil.

The Triune God Typified
by the Three Units of Five Hundred Shekels

In the compound ointment, there are five hundred shekels of myrrh, two hundred fifty shekels of cinnamon, two hundred fifty shekels of calamus, and five hundred shekels of cassia. In between the five hundred shekels of myrrh and the five hundred shekels of cassia are two items of two hundred fifty shekels. These two added together form one unit of five hundred shekels. Eventually, we may say that there are three units of five hundred shekels in the compound ointment. The middle unit is split into two parts. This is very meaningful. Among the Three of the Trinity, the Son, typified by the second unit of five hundred shekels, was "split," crucified, on the cross. The three units of five hundred shekels typify the Triune God, and the Triune God went to the cross in the second person of His Trinity, in the Son.

The Power for Responsibility

The four spices plus the oil are five elements. The five hundred and two hundred fifty shekels also involve the number five. The number five signifies responsibility. This means that the compound Spirit is the One who bears all responsibility. Without this ointment anointing us, we cannot do anything for God. We cannot be responsible for anything pertaining to God. But with this anointing Spirit, we surely have the capacity to bear any kind of responsibility for God's service.

The Compound Spirit for Anointing

The compound Spirit is the consummation of the processed, compounded Triune God. This Spirit is for anointing. Everything that is related to God's worship, to God's service, must be anointed by this compound Spirit. The compound ointment was used to anoint the tabernacle with all its furniture, the altar with all its utensils, the laver with its base, and the priests (Exo. 30:26-30). The function of the holy anointing oil as a compound ointment is to sanctify the things of God and the men of God, separating them from anything common and making them most holy for God's service.

The word *anointing* is used in the New Testament. First John 2:20 says that we have received the anointing, and verse 27 says that this anointing will teach us in all things. Paul told us in 2 Corinthians 1:21 that it is God who has anointed us and that God has attached us to Christ, the anointed One. Since we have been attached to Him, His anointing becomes ours. We are under the anointing of Christ.

The anointing is the moving of the compounded, ultimately consummated Spirit. The compound Spirit is moving within us, anointing us. When the ointment anoints us, all the elements of the ointment become our portion. Anointing can be compared to painting. Paint is a compound, a kind of ointment. When something is painted, the elements of the paint are applied to it. We are being anointed, painted, with the compound ointment, and all the elements of this ointment are being applied to our inward being. This anointing is taking place within us day by day.

THE MINGLED SPIRIT—THE DIVINE SPIRIT MINGLED WITH OUR HUMAN SPIRIT

The mingled spirit is the divine Spirit mingled with our human spirit (Rom. 8:4-6, 16; 1 Cor. 6:17). It is hard for Bible teachers to discern whether Paul is talking about the divine Spirit or our human spirit in Romans 8. Actually, Paul is talking about the mingled spirit. When Paul tells us to walk according to spirit in Romans 8:4 and to set our mind upon the spirit in verse 6, he is referring to the mingled spirit. To signify the mingled spirit, we may put a small letter *s* within a capital letter *S*. Romans 8:16 says that the Spirit witnesses with our spirit. The two spirits are working as one. First Corinthians 6:17 says that he who is joined to the Lord is one spirit. How wonderful it is that we are one spirit with the Lord! We are joined to the Lord, who is the Spirit, and we are one spirit with Him.

THE SEVEN SPIRITS—THE SEVENFOLD SPIRIT
TYPIFIED BY THE SEVEN LAMPS OF THE LAMPSTAND

The seven Spirits are the sevenfold Spirit, typified by the seven lamps of the lampstand (Rev. 1:4; 4:5; 5:6; Exo. 25:31, 37; Zech. 4:2, 10; 3:9). Matthew 28:19 says that we need to baptize the nations into the name of the Father, of the Son, and of the Holy Spirit. When Revelation 1:4 and 5 speak of the divine Trinity, the Spirit is referred to as "the seven Spirits who are before His throne." By comparing Revelation 1:4 and 5 with Matthew 28:19, we can realize that the seven Spirits are just the Holy Spirit. The seven Spirits are the Spirit of God because They are ranked among the Triune God in Revelation 1:4 and 5.

The seven Spirits are before the throne of God. The throne of God is for God's move in His administration, in His government. We may also say that the throne is for God's move in His economy. The word *economy* means arrangement, household administration, or household government. The seven Spirits actually are the one Spirit of God which is sevenfold for God's move to carry out God's administration. As seven is the number for completion in God's operation, so the seven Spirits must be for God's move on the earth. In essence and existence, God's Spirit is one; in the intensified function and work of God's operation. God's Spirit is sevenfold.

Revelation 4:5 says that the seven lamps of fire burning before the throne are the seven Spirits of God. These lamps are the seven lamps of the lampstand. In the tabernacle in the Old Testament, there was a lampstand. In existence it was one lampstand, but in function it was seven lamps. Revelation tells us that the seven lamps are the seven Spirits. Based upon this, we may say that the lampstand signifies the Triune God. The gold as the nature refers to the Father. The form of the lampstand refers to the Son as the very form. The seven lamps refer to the Holy Spirit as the expression.

Revelation 5:6 tells us that the seven Spirits of God are the seven eyes of the Lamb. Christ as the Lamb of God for our redemption has seven eyes. Some say that the Father, the Son, and the Spirit are separate. This is absolutely wrong. How could a person's eyes be separated from him? The Holy

Spirit is the eyes of Christ. Zechariah 4:10 tells us that these seven lamps are the seven eyes of the Lord. Then Zechariah 3:9 says that these eyes are the seven eyes of the stone. This stone is Christ.

Eyes are for observing and searching. Christ as the redeeming Lamb has seven observing and searching eyes for executing God's judgment upon the universe to fulfill God's eternal purpose, which will consummate in the building up of the New Jerusalem. Therefore, in Zechariah 3:9 He is prophesied as the stone, which is the topstone (4:7) with seven eyes for God's building. These seven eyes are the "seven Spirits of God, sent forth into all the earth" (Rev. 5:6), running "to and fro through the whole earth" (Zech. 4:10).

THE SPIRIT—THE CONSUMMATED SPIRIT AS THE CONSUMMATION OF THE PROCESSED TRIUNE GOD

The Spirit is the consummated Spirit as the consummation of the processed Triune God (John 7:39; 1 Pet. 1:2; Rev. 22:17a). Genesis 1:2 says that the Spirit of God brooded upon the face of the waters. At the end of the Bible, Revelation 22:17 refers to "the Spirit." This verse mentions the Spirit and the bride. The Spirit is the consummation of the processed Triune God, and the bride is the consummation of the transformed, tripartite man. The processed God marries the transformed man. The husband is triune, and the wife is tripartite. They match each other. The Triune God has been processed, and the tripartite man will have been transformed. God was processed by putting on man's nature, and man was transformed by partaking of God's nature. God took man's nature to get processed, and man took God's nature to get transformed. Man and God are married in their nature. God's nature becomes man's nature; man's nature becomes God's nature. The conclusion of the entire sixty-six books of the Bible is the marriage of a couple. This couple is the processed Triune God and the transformed tripartite man.

John 7:39 says that "the Spirit was not yet, because Jesus was not yet glorified." Jesus was glorified when He was resurrected (Luke 24:26). When Jesus was crucified and resurrected, He was glorified and the Triune God was consummated. After resurrection and in resurrection, the Lord Jesus came back to the disciples and told them to baptize people into the Triune God—the Father, the Son, and the Holy Spirit. The name of the Triune God was not revealed so completely until the resurrection of Christ was accomplished. It is in the resurrection of Christ that Christ became the life-giving Spirit, who is "the Spirit."

First Peter 1:2 also mentions "the Spirit." It says that we were chosen "according to the foreknowledge of God the Father, in sanctification of the Spirit, unto obedience and sprinkling of the blood of Jesus Christ." The Spirit's sanctification carries out the selection of God the Father that we may receive God the Son's redemption. The sanctification of the Spirit separates us from the world that we may enjoy God's full salvation. This Spirit is the consummated Spirit as the consummation of the processed Triune God.

CHAPTER THREE

THE SYMBOLS OF THE SPIRIT

(1)

Scripture Reading: Gen. 1:2 (ASV note); Deut. 32:11; Isa. 31:5; Matt. 3:16b; John 1:32; Psa. 45:7; Heb. 1:9; Isa. 61:1; Zech. 4:6,11,14 (Darby); Exo. 30:25-26; 1 John 2:20,27; 2 Cor. 1:21; Ezek. 1:4a; 37:9a; John 3:8; Acts 2:2; Ezek. 37:9b-10,14a; John 20:22; Exo. 14:20, 24; 40:34-38a; Num. 10:34; 1 Cor. 10:2; Ezek. 1:4b; Exo. 40:38b; Ezek. 1:4c; Acts 2:3-4; Ezek. 1:4d; Gen. 2:5; Deut. 11:14; Joel 2:23, 28-29; Hosea 6:3; Zech. 10:1; Acts 2:16-18; Exo. 17:6; John 4:10, 14; 7:38-39; Rev. 22:1, 17b; 21:6b; Gen. 2:10-14; Psa. 36:8; 46:4; Ezek. 47:1, 5, 7-9,12; Exo. 25:37; Zech. 4:2, 10b; Rev. 1:4c; 4:5b; 5:6

In this message we want to see fourteen symbols of the Spirit. These fourteen symbols can be divided into seven pairs. The first pair is the brooding bird and the dove. The second pair is the olive oil and the anointing ointment. The third pair is the wind and the breath. The fourth pair is the cloud and the fire. The fifth pair is the light and the rain. The sixth pair is the living water and the river of water of life. The last pair is the seven lamps of the lampstand and the seven eyes of the Lamb.

It is interesting to note that both the Old Testament and the New Testament begin with the Spirit as a bird and end with the Spirit as water. In the Old Testament, Genesis 1:2 says that the Spirit of God was brooding (as a bird) upon or over the death waters. In the New Testament, Matthew 3:16b and John 1:32 show us that the Spirit is as a dove. The last symbols of the Spirit in the Old Testament are the rain (Zech. 10:1) and the river of water of life (Ezek. 47:1, 5, 7-9, 12).

These symbols are concerning the water. Then the last symbol of the Spirit in the New Testament is the river of water of life (Rev. 22:1, 17b).

THE BROODING BIRD

Genesis 1:2 says, "The Spirit of God was brooding upon the face of the waters" (Gen. 1:2—ASV note). Brooding is for bringing something into life. In Genesis 1 the Spirit of God was brooding over the death waters to produce something of life out of death. The brooding of the Spirit brought in light. Without light, there is no life. After light was brought in, the plant life came into existence. Following this was the animal life with the birds, the fish, the cattle, and the creeping things. Eventually, the human life was created. Then the tree of life, denoting the divine life, the highest life, was presented to the human life. All of these different kinds of life came out of the brooding of the Spirit as the divine bird. The brooding of the Spirit brought forth life. This is the basic principle of the move of the Spirit today. Before we heard the gospel, we were dead just like the death waters. Then the Spirit of God came to brood over us, and that brooding produced life. The thought of the Lord as a brooding bird is also expressed in Deuteronomy 32:11 and Isaiah 31:5. Whenever the God of life comes to the ones in death, He comes as a brooding bird. He comes to brood over them to produce life.

THE DOVE

In John 1:29, John the Baptist said, "Behold, the Lamb of God." Then in verse 32, John said, "I beheld the Spirit descending as a dove out of heaven, and He abode upon Him." John introduced Jesus as a little lamb with a dove upon Him. The Lamb redeems, and the dove's work is to produce life. The redeeming Lamb is the life-producing dove. The Spirit as the brooding bird and as the dove is for the producing of life.

THE (OLIVE) OIL

The (olive) oil is another symbol of the Spirit (Psa. 45:7; Heb. 1:9; Isa. 61:1; Zech. 4:6, 11, 14—Darby). Psalm 45:7 says,

"God, thy God, hath anointed thee with the oil of gladness."
The oil of gladness is the Spirit of joy. God has anointed
Christ with the oil of gladness, the Spirit of joy. Now we need
to ask how we know that the olive oil symbolizes the Spirit.
We know this by comparing Isaiah 61:1 with Hebrews 1:9.
Isaiah 61:1 says, "The Spirit of the Lord Jehovah is upon me;
because Jehovah has anointed me." Hebrews 1:9 says that
God has anointed Christ "with the oil of exultant joy." The
Spirit with which Christ was anointed in Isaiah 61:1 is the oil
of exultant joy in Hebrews 1:9. This proves that the oil is the
anointing Spirit.

Zechariah is a wonderful book concerning Christ with His
Spirit. Zechariah 4 shows us the two olive trees on the right of
the lampstand and on its left (v. 11). The work of the lampstand is to shine with light, but for the lampstand to shine, it
needs the olive oil. Without the olive oil, the lampstand stops
working. Today it is the same with us. Revelation 1 tells us
that the churches are the lampstands. The work of the church
as the lampstand is to shine with light. For the churches to
shine forth light, there is the need of the Spirit. Zechariah 4:6
says, "Not by might, nor by power, but by my Spirit." The two
olive trees on the right and on the left of the lampstand are
full of oil (v. 12), full of the Spirit. Zechariah 4:14 tells us that
the two olive trees are the two sons of oil (Darby). The lampstand needs the Spirit. From all these verses, we can see that
the olive oil is a symbol of the Spirit, which the lampstand
needs to shine forth the light.

THE ANOINTING OINTMENT—
THE COMPOUND SPIRIT FOR ANOINTING

The Spirit is also symbolized by the anointing ointment,
which is the compound Spirit for anointing (Exo. 30:25-26;
1 John 2:20, 27; 2 Cor. 1:21). The difference between the oil
and the ointment is that the ointment is a compound. In
order to make an ointment, something of liquid is needed as
a base. Then some elements are added into the liquid and
compounded together. The Spirit that is working upon us and
within us is not only an oil but also an ointment. The four elements in the compound ointment in Exodus 30 are myrrh,

cinnamon, calamus, and cassia. These four elements are mingled together with olive oil. They are compounded together into one ointment.

Many Christians may know the Holy Spirit, but they do not have the realization of the compound Spirit. Before the incarnation of God, the Spirit of God had not been compounded with the elements of the Triune God's processes. But after God's incarnation and through Christ's crucifixion and resurrection, the Spirit of God became a compound Spirit. The element of the Spirit of God before God's incarnation was divinity, which is God Himself. Through God's incarnation, humanity was added to the Spirit. Through Christ's crucifixion, the all-inclusive death of Christ was added into the Spirit. Through His resurrection, the element of resurrection with its power was added into the Spirit. Now in the Spirit are divinity plus humanity plus death plus resurrection. All of these elements have been compounded together into an anointing ointment, which is the compound Spirit.

THE WIND

The Spirit is also symbolized by the wind (Ezek. 1:4a; 37:9a; John 3:8; Acts 2:2). The Hebrew word *ruach* can be translated spirit, wind, or breath. In Ezekiel 37, *ruach* is translated in these three ways. Ezekiel 1:4a says that a strong wind came out of the north. According to the Psalms, God dwells in the north (Psa. 48:2). When people go north, they say that they are going up, and when they go south, they say that they are going down. God is up, and Satan is down. This is the principle of the universe. A strong wind coming from the north means that the strong Spirit comes from the very God.

In Ezekiel 1:4 there are also the cloud, the fire, and the brightness, which is the light. The wind brought in the cloud, and in the cloud is the fire. Along with the fire is the brightness, which is the light. The wind, the cloud, the fire, and the light all refer to the Spirit.

In the New Testament, the Spirit is also symbolized by the wind. John 3:8 says, "The wind blows where it wills, and you hear the sound of it, but you do not know where it comes from

and where it is going; so is everyone who is born of the Spirit."
The Greek word *pneuma* is the word for wind and for spirit.
Whether it means the wind or the spirit depends upon the
context. The context here says that it blows and the sound of
it can be heard. This indicates that it is the wind. The Spirit
as the blowing wind brings God into us for our regeneration.

One of our co-workers was saved by the blowing of the
Spirit. Before he was saved, he was a member of the Nationalist party. At that time they considered that Christianity was
a tool of imperialism. Thus, this brother despised Christianity
to the uttermost. He considered it as a foreign religion used
by the imperialists. One day as he was sightseeing, he went to
a certain mountain where there was an idol temple. When
he entered this idol temple, to his surprise he saw a big Bible
that was opened to Psalm 1. When he read Psalm 1, he was
surprised at and inspired with what he read. He continued to
read the Bible in this idol temple, and eventually he was convicted of his sins, realizing that he was a sinner before God.
He wept and rolled on the ground repenting. The Spirit was a
strong wind that day to get him regenerated. He was saved by
the Lord, he withdrew from the Nationalist party, and he
eventually became one of our co-workers. His regeneration
was by the wind.

Others among us were not saved by such a strong wind of
the Spirit. The Spirit may have come to us as a gentle breeze.
Our confession may have been very gentle. We could have
simply prayed in this way: "Jesus, I love You. I am a sinner. I
believe in You, and I take You. Thank You, Lord Jesus." Many
of us were regenerated in a gentle way. Others have been
regenerated in a strong and even wild way. When they were
regenerated, they may have jumped, shouted, danced, or cried.
The Spirit as the wind in John 3:8 is mentioned in relation to
those who are regenerated, who are born of the Spirit.

THE BREATH

According to Ezekiel 37 the wind brings in the breath
(vv. 9b-10, 14a). In John 20:22 the Spirit as the breath was
breathed as life into the disciples for their life. After His resurrection, the Lord came back to the disciples to breathe into

them. John 20:22 says, "He breathed into them and said to them, Receive the Holy Spirit." His breath is the Spirit.

THE CLOUD

The cloud is another symbol of the Spirit (Exo. 14:20, 24; 40:34-38a; Num. 10:34; 1 Cor. 10:2; Ezek. 1:4b). In Ezekiel 1:4 there is the thought that the wind brings in the cloud. Exodus tells us that when the Israelites desired to go out of Egypt, Pharaoh would not let them go. Therefore, the Spirit had to come in to fight for them. At that time the Spirit came as a pillar of cloud. During the day the Lord went before them in a pillar of a cloud to lead them. At night the pillar of cloud was a pillar of fire to give them light (Exo. 13:21-22). Exodus tells us that this pillar of cloud and of fire stood between the camp of the Egyptians and the camp of Israel (14:20, 24). Exodus and Numbers tell us that the cloud covered the tent of meeting (Exo. 40:34-38a; Num. 10:34). The cloud became the covering, the protection, of the tabernacle. That cloud was the presence of Jehovah, and that presence was God Himself as the Spirit overshadowing His people.

THE FIRE

According to Ezekiel 1:4, the wind brings in the cloud, and within the cloud is the fire. In Exodus the fire within the pillar of cloud made it a pillar of fire. The fire is in the cloud. Also, Acts 2 shows us that when the Holy Spirit was poured out upon the disciples, tongues as of fire sat on each one of them (vv. 3-4). Tongues as of fire signify the function of the Spirit. A tongue is a symbol of speaking, symbolizing that God's economical Spirit of power is mostly for speaking. He is the speaking Spirit. The fire symbolizes burning power for purging and motivating in God's economical move.

THE LIGHT

The fire brings in the light, the "brightness" (Ezek. 1:4d). The Spirit is symbolized by the light. Wherever fire is, light is there. When a candle is burning with fire, that burning gives light. The Holy Spirit is fire and also light.

THE RAIN—
THE FORMER RAIN AND THE LATTER RAIN

The Spirit is symbolized by the rain—the former rain and the latter rain (Gen. 2:5; Deut. 11:14; Joel 2:23, 28-29; Hosea 6:3; Zech. 10:1; Acts 2:16-18). Frequently, lightning accompanies the rain. Therefore, there is "fire" with the rain. In the same way, if we have the fire of the Spirit, the rain will come.

The Old Testament refers to the former rain and the latter rain. The former rain was in the fall, and the latter rain was in the spring. The former rain and the latter rain both refer to the Spirit in the right season. Joel 2:23 says that the Lord gives the former rain, the autumn rain, and the latter rain, the spring rain. Then in verses 28 and 29, the Lord says twice that He will pour out His Spirit. The pouring out of the Spirit is the fulfillment of the former rain and the latter rain. The pouring out of the Spirit on the day of Pentecost was the former rain. Then at the end of this age, God will pour out His Spirit again. That will be the latter rain. This latter rain is prophesied of in Zechariah 12:10. This verse says, "And I will pour upon the house of David, and upon the inhabitants of Jerusalem, the spirit of grace and of supplications: and they shall look upon me whom they have pierced, and they shall mourn for him, as one mourneth for his only son, and shall be in bitterness for him, as one that is in bitterness for his firstborn." At Christ's coming, the Lord will pour out His Spirit upon the children of Israel, and they all will repent.

With the Jews there are the two rains. When Peter stood up and spoke on the day of Pentecost, that was the fulfillment of Joel 2. But Peter did not say there would be another pouring out of the Spirit at the end of the age. This pouring out of the Spirit is prophesied in Zechariah 12. God will pour out His Spirit upon the children of Israel, they will repent, and all Israel will be saved. This will be the latter rain to the Jews. This indicates that God gives us His Spirit in the right season. Both the former rain and the latter rain are given at the season of need. Spring and autumn are both seasons for farming, so both seasons need the rain.

THE LIVING WATER

The living water is a symbol of the Spirit (Exo. 17:6; John 4:10, 14; 7:38-39). Exodus 17:6 speaks of the living water coming out of the cleft rock. First Corinthians 10:4 tells us that the cleft rock was a rock that followed the children of Israel. The living water that flowed out of the cleft rock typifies the Spirit as our all-inclusive drink. In John 4 the Lord Jesus told the Samaritan woman that He had the living water to give her. Then in John 7 He said that rivers of living water would flow out of the innermost being of His believers. Out of our innermost being flows a river of patience, a river of comfort, a river of power, etc. Rivers of living water are the many flows of the different aspects of life of the one unique river of water of life (Rev. 22:1).

THE RIVER OF WATER OF LIFE

The river of water of life is another symbol of the Spirit (Rev. 22:1, 17b; 21:6b; Gen. 2:10-14; Psa. 36:8; 46:4; Ezek. 47:1, 5, 7-9, 12). This river of water of life is a symbol of God in Christ as the Spirit flowing Himself into His redeemed people to be their life and life supply. In Revelation 22:1 the water of life becomes a river proceeding out of the throne of God and of the Lamb to supply and saturate the entire New Jerusalem. Therefore, as the ultimate consummation of the processed Triune God, the Spirit as the river of water of life is the flow of the processed Triune God with Himself as the water of life to satisfy His chosen people that He may have an eternal manifestation to express Himself for eternity.

THE SEVEN LAMPS OF THE LAMPSTAND— THE SEVEN SPIRITS BEFORE THE THRONE OF GOD

The Spirit is symbolized by the seven lamps of the lampstand, which are the seven Spirits before the throne of God (Exo. 25:37; Zech. 4:2, 10b; Rev. 1:4c; 4:5b). The lampstand is mentioned in Exodus, Zechariah, and Revelation. God's people on this earth should be like a lampstand. In Exodus 25, the lampstand signifies Christ. In Zechariah 4 the lampstand signifies the people of Israel. Finally, the lampstands in Revelation 1 signify the churches (v. 20), which are the enlargement of Christ.

The lampstand has seven lamps, and these seven lamps are the Spirit for the expression of the Triune God. The lampstand has three aspects: the gold essence, the form, and the expression. The essence is the Father, the form is the Son, and the expression is the Spirit. Zechariah 4 reveals that the seven lamps refer to the Spirit. Then in Revelation 4:5 the seven lamps of fire burning before God's throne are the seven Spirits of God. The seven lamps of the lampstand are the seven Spirits before the throne of God to execute God's administration on the whole earth.

THE SEVEN EYES OF THE LAMB—
THE SEVEN SPIRITS OF GOD
SENT FORTH INTO ALL THE EARTH

In Revelation 5:6 the Spirit is symbolized by the seven eyes of the Lamb, which are the seven Spirits of God sent forth into all the earth. The seven eyes of the Lamb are also the seven lamps of the lampstand. The lamps are for enlightening and burning; the eyes are for watching and observing and also for infusing and transfusing. As the redeeming Lamb, Christ has seven watching and observing eyes for the carrying out of God's administration. These seven eyes are also transfusing all that the Lamb is into our being so that we may become the same as He is. Today the seven Spirits are moving to accomplish God's building for the fulfillment of His New Testament economy.

CHAPTER FOUR

THE SYMBOLS OF THE SPIRIT

(2)

Scripture Reading: Gen. 1:2 (ASV note); Deut. 32:11; Isa. 31:5; Matt. 3:16b; John 1:32; Psa. 45:7; Heb. 1:9; Isa. 61:1; Zech. 4:6, 11, 14 (Darby); Exo. 30:25-26; 1 John 2:20, 27; 2 Cor. 1:21; Ezek. 1:4a; 37:9a; John 3:8; Acts 2:2; Ezek. 37:9b-10, 14a; John 20:22; Exo. 14:20, 24; 40:34-38a; Num. 10:34; 1 Cor. 10:2; Ezek. 1:4b; Exo. 40:38b; Ezek. 1:4c; Acts 2:3-4; Ezek. 1:4d; Gen. 2:5; Deut. 11:14; Joel 2:23, 28-29; Hosea 6:3; Zech. 10:1; Acts 2:16-18; Exo. 17:6; John 4:10, 14; 7:38-39; Rev. 22:1, 17b; 21:6b; Gen. 2:10-14; Psa. 36:8; 46:4; Ezek. 47:1, 5, 7-9, 12; Exo. 25:37; Zech. 4:2, 10b; Rev. 1:4c; 4:5b; 5:6

In this message we want to see more concerning the application of the fourteen symbols of the Spirit pointed out in message three. In that message we saw that these fourteen symbols can be considered in seven pairs: the brooding bird and the dove; the (olive) oil and the anointing ointment; the wind and the breath; the cloud and the fire; the light and the rain; the living water and the river of water of life; the seven lamps of the lampstand and the seven eyes of the Lamb.

The first pair is the brooding bird (Gen. 1:2) and the dove (Matt. 3:16). We need to ask why the first symbol of the Spirit in both the Old and New Testaments is a bird. This is the way to study the holy Word. We should never take anything in the Word for granted. The next pair is the oil and the anointing ointment. In the good Samaritan's care for the dying one, he poured oil and wine on his wounds (Luke 10:34). This indicates that the oil is for soothing and for healing. The very God, who is the Spirit, is all the time soothing and healing us.

The wind and the breath are the third pair, and the cloud and the fire are the fourth pair. Within the cloud is the fire. This may sound strange, but actually it is common. Quite often, lightning is in the cloud. When the lightning is in the cloud, the fire is in the cloud. With the fire there is the light, another symbol of the Spirit. On a dark night, lightning issues in light. The Spirit as the light is paired with the Spirit as the rain. On a rainy day, there are the cloud, the lightning (the fire), the light, and the rain. The cloud, the fire, the light, and the rain are all symbols of the Spirit. Then the rain gives us the water, and the water forms a river. This brings us to the next pair of the symbols of the Spirit—the living water and the river of water of life. An abundance of flowing water is a river.

The last pair of the symbols of the Spirit is the seven lamps of the lampstand and the seven eyes of the Lamb. The beginning and the end of the Old and New Testaments are the same concerning the Spirit. Both the Old and New Testaments begin with the Spirit as a bird and end with the Spirit as the seven lamps of the lampstand, as the seven eyes, and as water. In Zechariah the Spirit is symbolized by the seven lamps as the seven eyes of Jehovah (4:2, 10), and the Spirit is also symbolized by the rain (10:1). In Revelation, the last book of the New Testament, the Spirit is symbolized by the seven lamps of the lampstand (1:4c; 4:5b), the seven eyes of the Lamb (5:6), and the river of water of life (22:1).

THE ANOINTING OINTMENT

As we have pointed out, the Spirit as the oil (Heb. 1:9) is for soothing and healing. The Spirit as ointment is for anointing (Exo. 30:25-26; 1 John 2:20, 27; 2 Cor. 1:21). In the Gospels, the Lord Jesus healed a certain blind man in a particular way. The Word says that the Lord Jesus "spat on the ground and made clay of the spittle and anointed his eyes with the clay" (John 9:6). The Lord anointed the blind man's eyes with a kind of ointment. An ointment is always composed of more than one element, and it is for the purpose of anointing. The Lord's Spirit is the anointing Spirit, the anointing ointment. Every ointment has a number of ingredients, or elements. In eternity past, God was only one element, but one day He began to be compounded. First, God was compounded with man. One day He entered the womb of a virgin, and He stayed there for nine months. Divinity was compounded with humanity. God was born as a man, and this man was a compounded man. Jesus was a compound of God and man.

Jesus, the unique God-man, walked on this earth for thirty-three and a half years, and then He entered into death. He was compounded with death. A piece of cloth that has been put into dye is compounded with the dye. If the cloth is white and the dye is blue, the cloth becomes a blue cloth. When the Lord Jesus went to the cross, His death was like a dye with which He was compounded. Thus, the very God was compounded with humanity and death. After three days He came out of death and was compounded with another element, the element of resurrection. After forty days, He ascended into the third heavens, and He was compounded with the element of ascension. Thus, we can say that our God today is a compound of five elements: God, man, death, resurrection, and ascension. Our God today is the very compound Spirit, who is the consummation of the processed Triune God. Our God today is the top compound. He is the ointment. God Himself is the oil, and this oil has been compounded with four kinds of "spices": man, death, resurrection, and ascension. Such a compound ointment is for the purpose of anointing.

Anointing means painting. When something is painted, the elements of the paint are added to it. Obviously, if a table is painted with green paint it becomes green. A certain table may be coated with many coats of paint. All of us may be likened to tables who are being painted with the processed Triune God. We have been painted with the processed Triune God, but how many coats of paint have we received? We need to open ourselves to the Lord to receive more of His painting. His anointing. The New Testament tells us that we have received the anointing. This means that we have received the painting. This anointing, this painting, is still going on within us.

Christ as the Spirit is the divine paint. God is painting us with Himself as the Spirit. Some have a Pentecostal concept that they need to pray and fast for three days to receive the Spirit. But according to our experience, our receiving of the Spirit is for us to be painted with the Spirit. Today the consummated Spirit of God as the consummation of the processed Triune God is being applied to us all the time.

As we have seen, the ingredients in this compound Spirit are God, man, death, resurrection, and ascension. Galatians 2:20 says that we have been crucified with Christ, but we may still be so strong in our disposition and our character. In our experience we are short of the death of Christ. How can we get this death? This wonderful death is an ingredient in the compound Spirit. To receive this ingredient, we need more painting. On the one hand, God uses the people close to us and the environment to help paint us. On the other hand, our Lord paints us directly. He is a great painter, who paints us with Himself. We need to pray to God, to contact Him. We need to approach God and stay with Him to fellowship with Him. The longer we stay with Him, the more He paints us.

In the divine paint, the compound Spirit, there is the ingredient of the death of Christ. The more we contact the Lord, the more His death gets into us, and this death kills us. The compound Spirit is like an all-inclusive drink with all kinds of ingredients. When we pray regularly, the death of Christ, as an ingredient of the compound Spirit, becomes a spiritual medication to us.

First John 2 tells us that we have received an anointing (vv. 20, 27), and that anointing is the moving of the compound Spirit as the anointing ointment. Within this ointment are the ingredients of Christ's divinity, humanity, all-inclusive death, germinating resurrection, and transcending ascension. These ingredients will transform us. We need to remain in the enjoyment of the anointing of the compound Spirit.

THE WIND, THE BREATH, THE CLOUD, AND THE FIRE

We Christians also need to experience the Spirit as the wind (John 3:8; Acts 2:2). The wind brings us the Spirit as the breath (John 20:22). The Spirit as the breath refreshes us and makes us new inwardly. The wind also brings us the

Spirit as the cloud (Exo. 14:20, 24; 1 Cor. 10:2). Spiritually speaking, the Spirit as the cloud is the presence of God. God is symbolized by the cloud. When the tabernacle was erected, the cloud covered it (Exo. 40:34-38a). That covering, protecting, guiding cloud was God Himself. The spiritual wind brings God's presence to us. If we have the cloud, we have God with us. We may even say that the cloud is the condensation of the Lord's presence. Within the cloud is the fire that burns and enlightens. Whenever we enjoy the Spirit as the cloud, we also have the Spirit as the fire to burn us and enlighten us (Ezek. 1:4c; Acts 2:3-4).

THE LIGHT AND THE RAIN

The Spirit is also the light as the issue of the fire (Ezek. 1:4d) and the spiritual rain (Hosea 6:3). This rain comes to us through the Spirit as the wind, the breath, the cloud, the fire, and the light. On the day of Pentecost, the outpouring of the Holy Spirit was the Spirit as the rain (Acts 2:16-18). Genesis 2:5 tells us that at that time there was no rain because there was no man to till the ground. When man comes to till the ground, the rain comes. As we are laboring in the Lord, the Spirit as the wind will come. Then the wind will bring us the breath, the breath will bring us the cloud, the cloud will bring us the fire, the fire will bring us the light, and eventually the light will bring us the rain.

THE LIVING WATER
AND THE RIVER OF WATER OF LIFE

The Spirit is also symbolized by the living water (Exo. 17:6; John 4:10, 14; 7:38-39). The Spirit as the rain issues in the living water. This living water becomes the river of water of life. Ezekiel 47 presents a picture of the Spirit as the river of water of life. The depth of the river begins at the ankles and then rises to the knees and to the loins. Eventually, it becomes a river to swim in, a river that cannot be passed over (vv. 3-5).

In the Bible there is the line of the Spirit as a river. Genesis 2:10-14 says that a river went out of Eden to water the garden, and this river was parted into four heads toward the four directions of the earth. Psalm 36:8 says that the Lord shall make us to drink of the river of His pleasures. Psalm 46:4 says that there is a river that makes the city of God glad. Then in John 7 the Lord Jesus told us that those who believe in Him will have rivers of living water flowing out of their innermost being (vv. 38-39). The one river of water of life flows out of us as many rivers, just as the river in Genesis 2 was parted into four rivers. Finally, in the book of Revelation, there is the consummated river (22:1). This is the river that flows out of the throne of God to water the entire New Jerusalem, to supply the entire body of God's chosen and redeemed people. The river is the consummated Spirit, and the consummated Spirit is the consummated God. The river is the flowing out of the consummated and processed Triune God to be our drink for our enjoyment.

First Corinthians 12:13 says that we have all been baptized in one Spirit into one Body and that now we are drinking of this one Spirit. The Spirit as the river of water of life is for drinking. On the one hand, the consummated God is the outpoured Spirit for our baptism. On the other hand, the same consummated Spirit is the river that is good for us to drink.

The symbols of the Spirit are illustrations to portray how our God, after being processed and consummated, becomes our enjoyment. The Bible uses all the symbols to describe and to portray how God becomes so enjoyable and so available to us through all of His processes. He becomes the bird to brood over us for God's move. He has become the oil to soothe us and to heal us. He has become the ointment to anoint us. He has also become the wind, the breath, the cloud, the fire, the light, the rain, the water, and the river for our enjoyment. All these symbols of the Spirit portray our enjoyable God.

THE SEVEN LAMPS OF THE LAMPSTAND
AND THE SEVEN EYES OF THE LAMB

The Spirit is also symbolized by the seven lamps of the lampstand, which are the seven Spirits before the throne of God (Exo. 25:37; Zech. 4:2, 10b; Rev. 1:4c; 4:5b), and by the seven eyes of the Lamb, which are the seven Spirits of God sent forth into all the earth (Rev. 5:6). The Spirit of God has been intensified sevenfold. It is like a seven-way lamp. I have seen three-way lamps before, but I have never seen a seven-way lamp. The Spirit of God today is like a seven-way lamp with intensified light. Our spiritual lamp is sevenfold intensified. This sevenfold intensified lamp is for shining, for enlightening, and for searching. The consummated Spirit is the sevenfold lamp to shine, enlighten, and search. These seven lamps are the seven eyes of the Redeemer, the Lamb. Eyes are for observing, searching, and infusing. The Lamb redeemed us with a purpose. For Him to carry out His purpose, He needs seven eyes to observe us, to search us, and to infuse us with all that He is. These seven eyes are the seven Spirits of God sent forth into all the earth to carry out God's purpose, God's economy.

We have to enjoy our processed Triune God as the consummated Spirit in all these aspects. We need to study these aspects of the Spirit, and we have to experience and be constituted with the Spirit in all these aspects.

CHAPTER FIVE

THE FUNCTIONS OF THE SPIRIT

(1)

Scripture Reading: Gen. 6:3; Psa. 51:10-12; Isa. 42:1; 61:1; Ezek. 36:27; 37:14; Zech. 4:6; 12:10

IN THE OLD TESTAMENT

In this message we want to fellowship concerning the functions of the Spirit in the Old Testament. God carries out and accomplishes things as the Spirit. The Spirit of God is actually the Spirit as God. The Spirit of Jehovah is the Spirit as Jehovah. The Spirit is God in action. When God does something, He does it as the Spirit.

Life-producing by Brooding

The first function of the Spirit as revealed in the Old Testament is the function of life-producing by brooding (Gen. 1:2). The record of Genesis 1 concerning God's creation is a record of the producing of life. God created the heavens and the earth, and the earth became waste and void. Then the Spirit of God came to brood over the death waters with the intention of producing life. As a result of the brooding of the Spirit, life was produced. First, the plant life was produced (Gen. 1:11-12). The plant life is for beautifying the earth, but it is also for food. Genesis 2 tells us that the trees are good for food (v. 9). The plant life is food for the animal life. After the plant life was produced, the animal life was created. This animal life includes the birds, the aquatic animals, the cattle, and the creeping things (Gen. 1:20-25). The animal life is for the human life. Eventually, the human life is for the divine life, the highest life. The record of God's creation is actually a record of life-producing by the brooding of the Spirit. The brooding of the Spirit as God produced life for the fulfillment of God's purpose.

Today in the new creation, the Spirit is also brooding for the producing of life. God created man, but man, like the earth, eventually became "waste and void." Then the Spirit of God comes to brood over man. This brooding function of the Spirit of God always goes along with the preaching of the gospel. When we preach the gospel, the Spirit is brooding to produce life in the unbelievers.

Striving with or Ruling in Fallen Man

The Spirit also functioned to strive with or rule in fallen man (Gen. 6:3). Man fell by the time of Genesis 3, and he continued to fall. Therefore, there was a struggle between the Spirit and fallen man. Because the fallen man was still falling, the Spirit was striving with him. God's Spirit was striving against man's rebellion. The Hebrew word for striving here could also be translated rule in. God's striving with man implies His ruling in man. In Genesis 6 a point was reached when the Spirit of God would strive with man no longer. Eventually, man became so corrupted that God had to judge the earth with a flood. The judgment of the flood came in because of the unbridled corruption of man.

Filling Man in Wisdom, Understanding, Knowledge, and Skill

Although the situation with man had reached a point where the Spirit of God would no longer strive with him, God would never give up man. Therefore, God came to man to call him, to redeem him, and to rescue him from his fallen situation. After God brought the children of Israel into the wilderness, the Spirit, who was brooding over and striving with man, became the filling Spirit. God filled man with the Spirit of God in wisdom, understanding, knowledge, and skill (Exo. 31:3; 35:31; Deut. 34:9). The Spirit filling man "in" these items means that the Spirit is these items. The filling Spirit that fills us is the Spirit as wisdom, knowledge, understanding, and skill. In the Old Testament, the people who were filled with the Spirit as wisdom, understanding, knowledge, and skill were the builders of the tabernacle. (For more fellowship concerning this, see Life-study of Exodus, message one hundred seventy, pp. 1803-1811.)

Prophesying

Another function of the Spirit is for prophesying (Num. 11:25, 29; 24:2-4; 1 Sam. 10:6, 10; 19:20, 23; 2 Sam. 23:2; 2 Chron. 15:1; 20:14; 24:20; Ezek. 11:4-5; Zech. 7:12). Today the most needful thing among us is prophesying. The practice of prophesying was exalted by Paul in 1 Corinthians 14. He indicated that prophesying was the excelling gift for the building up of the Body of Christ (vv. 4b, 12). All the verses we have listed above related to prophesying show that it is the most needful function of the Spirit as God in the Old Testament. Even in the Old Testament, prophesying is the most needful function. To prophesy is to speak God, to speak for God, and to speak forth God. We have to learn how to speak God, to speak for God, and to speak forth God.

Warring

The brooding Spirit, the striving Spirit, the filling Spirit, and the prophesying Spirit are also the warring Spirit (Judg. 3:10; 6:34; 11:29; 13:25; 14:6, 19; 15:14). The warring Spirit is the Spirit who fights against God's enemy.

Anointing with Power

In the Old Testament, the anointing of the Spirit is mainly for power (1 Sam. 16:13). But in the New Testament, the anointing is for us to enjoy all the riches of God. Power is one of the many attributes of God. In the New Testament, the anointing brings us all of God's attributes. In a previous message, we saw the Spirit typified by the compound ointment in Exodus 30. The Spirit as the compound ointment anoints us with all the elements of the consummated Triune God.

Carrying Man

First Kings 18:12 and 2 Kings 2:16 both show the

function of the Spirit in carrying man. In 1 Kings 18:12 Obadiah, fearing that Elijah would be carried away by the Spirit of the Lord, said, "And it shall come to pass, as soon as I am gone from thee, that the Spirit of the Lord shall carry thee whither I know not." Second Kings 2:16 also refers to Elijah being carried away by the Spirit as God.

Clothing

First Chronicles 12:18 reveals the Spirit as clothing— "Then the Spirit clothed Amasai..." (lit.). The Spirit as clothing is also revealed in Luke 24:49, where the Lord said, "Stay in the city until you are clothed with power from on high." The clothing of the Spirit upon man is man's uniform, not only for power but also for authority. Policemen wear a uniform, and their uniform gives them the authority. People will obey the orders of someone clothed in a police uniform. If the policeman did not have a uniform, however, who would listen to him? His uniform gives him the authority. When a uniformed policeman tells a person to stop his car, that person will stop. When the disciples were clothed with power from on high, they were clothed with the strongest and highest uniform. They were powerful and full of authority.

Man-creating and Life-giving

The Spirit also has the function of man-creating and life-giving (Job 33:4; Psa. 104:30; Mal. 2:15). Job 33:4 says, "The Spirit of God hath made me, and the breath of the Almighty hath given me life." This verse refers us back to Genesis 2:7, which says, "And the Lord God formed man of the dust of the ground, and breathed into his nostrils the breath of life; and man became a living soul." God formed man's body of the dust of the ground. The body of man is not the man himself. When a person dies, we say that he is gone even though his body is still with us. This indicates that a man's body is not the man himself. After the formation of man's body, God breathed the breath of life into man. That breathing was the creating of man. When the breath of life was breathed into man's nostrils, man became a living soul. When the Bible speaks of man, it refers to man as a "soul." Exodus 1:5 says, "And all the

souls that came out of the loins of Jacob were seventy souls."
Souls in this verse is synonymous with persons. Man is a
living soul. The breathing of the breath of life into man's body
was the creating of man, the making of man. This creating
goes together with life-giving. The Spirit is a man-creating
and life-giving Spirit.

Leading Man to Do the Will of God

The Spirit also leads man to do the will of God (Psa.
143:10). Many people are working for themselves, not for
God's will. The ones who are under the leading of the Spirit as
God are being led to do the will of God.

Giving Man a Right Spirit and a Willing Spirit

The Spirit functions to give man a right spirit and a willing spirit (Psa. 51:10-12). Psalm 51 is David's prayer after he
fell, repented, and came back to God. He prayed that the Lord
would give him a right spirit and a willing spirit. Much of the
time during the day our spirit may not be right. If someone
accidentally spills something at the dining table where we
are eating, do we have a right spirit? We may have a spirit
that condemns the person for being careless. This means that
our spirit is not right. Sometimes our spirit may be right but
not so willing. We may have a spirit which is right for going
out to preach the gospel, yet we may not have the morale.
This simply means that we do not have a willing spirit. When
our spirit is willing, we have the morale. We must confess that
we do not have anything in or of ourselves to have a right
spirit or a willing spirit. Therefore, we must pray, "Lord, give
me a right spirit and a willing spirit." Only the Spirit as God
can make our human spirit right and willing.

Giving Man Wisdom and Understanding, Counsel and Might, Knowledge and the Fear of Jehovah

The Spirit gives man wisdom and understanding, counsel
and might, knowledge and the fear of Jehovah (Isa. 11:2). The
one Spirit has these six attributes. Only the Spirit as God can
give us these wonderful attributes.

Outpouring upon Man

In the Old Testament, the Spirit also functioned to be out-poured upon man (Isa. 32:15; 44:3; Ezek. 39:29; Joel 2:28-29; Zech. 12:10). The Spirit is the outpouring Spirit. Joel 2:28-29 prophesied that the Lord would pour out His Spirit upon all flesh. This pouring out of the Spirit was fulfilled as the former rain on the day of Pentecost and will be fulfilled as the latter rain in Zechariah 12:10 when the Jews will repent at the Lord's coming back (Joel 2:23). Isaiah 32:15 says, "Until the Spirit be poured upon us from on high, and the wilderness be a fruitful field, and the fruitful field be counted for a forest." This verse says that the outpouring of the Spirit makes the wilderness fruitful. Thus, the outpouring of the Spirit is for the producing of life.

Gathering People

The Spirit functions to gather people. Isaiah 34:16 says, "Seek ye out of the book of Jehovah, and read: no one of these shall be missing, none shall want her mate; for my mouth, it hath commanded, and his Spirit, it hath gathered them" (ASV). It is not so easy for us to be gathered. But the Spirit as God is the gathering Spirit. He gathers man. Without the urging of the Spirit within us, we would not come to the meet-ings of the church. If we do not follow this urging fully, we may come to the meetings, but we will not come on time. We need the gathering Spirit.

Sending the Prophet

The Spirit is also the sending Spirit. Isaiah 48:16 says, "Come ye near unto me, hear ye this; I have not spoken in secret from the beginning; from the time that it was, there am I: and now the Lord God, and his Spirit, hath sent me." Now we need to ask who "me" is in this verse. Actually, when we trace the antecedent of "me" in this verse back to verse one, we can see that the sender is the sent one. This is similar to Zechariah 2:8-11, which reveals that the Lord of hosts sent the Lord of hosts.

Anointing for Gospel Preaching

The Spirit anoints man for the preaching of the gospel (Isa. 61:1; 42:1). Isaiah 42:1 says the Lord will come as the slave of Jehovah, and the Spirit of Jehovah will be upon Him. Isaiah 61:1 tells us that the Spirit of Jehovah who is on the slave of Jehovah is the anointing oil. This verse says, "The Spirit of the Lord God is upon me; because the Lord hath anointed me to preach good tidings unto the meek; he hath sent me to bind up the brokenhearted, to proclaim liberty to the captives, and the opening of the prison to them that are bound." This verse was fulfilled when Jehovah anointed the Lord Jesus with His Spirit (Luke 4:18-19).

Grieving for People and Giving Rest to People

Isaiah 63:10 and 14 unveil that the Spirit who works in so many ways is also the grieving Spirit and the rest-giving Spirit. When we grieve Him, He grieves for us. He is the One who also gives us rest. The grieving One is the rest-giving One. We may grieve the Spirit, and the Spirit grieves for us. Then we do not have rest. Eventually, once we confess our failure to the Lord and repent, the grieving Spirit becomes the rest-giving Spirit.

Moving in God's Move

The book of Ezekiel strongly reveals that the Spirit is moving in God's move (1:12, 20; 2:2; 3:12, 14, 24; 8:3; 11:1, 24; 37:1; 43:5). In Ezekiel 1 there is a vision of the four living creatures with the four wheels. This means that God is moving among His creatures. Ezekiel 1:12 says, "And they went every one straight forward: whither the spirit was to go, they went; and they turned not when they went." Verse 20 says, "Whithersoever the spirit was to go, they went, thither was their spirit to go; and the wheels were lifted up over against them: for the spirit of the living creature was in the wheels." Ezekiel 1 gives us a vision of how God is moving on this earth. In this move of God, the Spirit moves. For more fellowship concerning this, I would encourage you to read the book entitled *The Visions of Ezekiel.*

When we go out to visit people for the preaching of the gospel, we have to realize that the Spirit motivated and moved us to do this. The Spirit moves us, and then we move. In our going is the moving Spirit. The Spirit is moving in our move. When we knock on doors for the preaching of the gospel, the Spirit is there. Within our move to preach the gospel, there is an inner move. The outer move is ours, and the inner move is the Spirit's.

Causing Man to Keep God's Statutes and Ordinances

The Spirit causes man to keep God's statutes and ordinances (Ezek. 36:27). The law has only ten commandments. Besides these ten commandments, Exodus gives us a lot of subordinate items. Statutes and ordinances are subordinate items of the law. Statutes tell us not to do certain things. Ordinances are statutes which are given with a judgment or punishment if we disobey them. Exodus 20 gives us the law, and chapters twenty-one through twenty-three give us the supplementary items of the law, the statutes and ordinances. We have no power to keep God's statutes and ordinances. The Spirit gives us the strength and causes us to keep them.

Enlivening the Dead

Ezekiel 37:14 reveals that the Spirit enlivens the dead. The Spirit comes to enliven all the dead bones, so the Spirit is the enlivening Spirit.

Giving People Power, Judgment, and Might

The Spirit gives people power, judgment, and might. Micah 3:8 says, "But truly I am full of power by the Spirit of the Lord, and of judgment, and of might, to declare unto Jacob his transgression, and to Israel his sin." Zechariah 4:6 says, "Not by might, nor by power, but by my Spirit, saith the Lord of hosts." It is not by might nor by power, but by the Spirit of Jehovah that we can perform something for Him.

Abiding among God's People

The Spirit of God also has the function of abiding among

God's people (Hag. 2:5). He abides with us. We should not think that His abiding with us does not require strength. Could we stay with someone moment by moment all the time? This would be exhausting. We need to be alone. We need some privacy. But the abiding Spirit always abides with His people. Abiding is an ability and a function. The abiding Spirit never leaves us.

Grace-giving and Supplicating

Zechariah 12:10 shows that the Spirit is the grace-giving and supplicating Spirit. At the time of the Lord's coming back, the Spirit will be grace to the repenting Israel so that they will be able to supplicate, to pray, to petition God by the Spirit. That outpouring of the Spirit talked about in Zechariah 12:10 will be the Spirit as the latter rain.

Thank the Lord for the functions of the Spirit in the Old Testament. In His gracious action, God acts as the Spirit.

CHAPTER SIX

THE FUNCTIONS OF THE SPIRIT

(2)

Scripture Reading: Matt. 1:18b, 20b; 3:11c; 28:19; Mark 1:8; Luke 3:16; John 1:33; Matt. 3:16b; Luke 3:22; John 1:32; Matt. 4:1; Luke 4:1b; Matt. 10:20; Mark 13:11; Luke 12:12; Matt. 12:18, 28a; 25:4, 8-9; Mark 1:12; Luke 1:15b, 41b, 67, 35; 2:27-29, 25-26; 4:1a, 14a; 11:20; 24:19; 4:18a; 11:11-13; 15:8; John 3:5-6, 8, 34; 6:63; 7:38-39; 14:16; 15:26a; 16:7; 14:17a; 15:26b; 16:13a; 14:17b, 26; 15:26c; 16:8, 13-15; 20:22

IN THE NEW TESTAMENT—THE FOUR GOSPELS

In message five we saw the functions of the Spirit in the Old Testament. In this message we want to see the functions of the Spirit in the four Gospels of the New Testament. Many more functions of the Spirit are revealed in the New Testament than in the Old Testament. The Gospel of John reveals more aspects of the Spirit than each of the synoptic Gospels, Matthew, Mark, and Luke. These three Gospels are called synoptic because they correspond closely to one another.

Begetting

The first function of the Spirit in the New Testament is the function of begetting (Matt. 1:18b, 20b). Matthew 1:20b says, "That which is begotten in her is of the Holy Spirit." Something was begotten in Mary's womb of the Holy Spirit. The Holy Spirit is the Spirit that begets. The entire Triune God was begotten of the Spirit in Mary's womb. God was begotten in man. This is the greatest wonder and miracle in the whole universe! From the first day of Mary's pregnancy,

God was in her womb. According to the natural principle of God's creation, He stayed there for nine months. Matthew 1:18 and 20 indicate that the divine essence out of the Holy Spirit had been generated in Mary's womb before she delivered the Child Jesus.

Baptizing

The Spirit also has the function of baptizing (Matt. 3:11c; 28:19; Mark 1:8; Luke 3:16; John 1:33). Actually, according to the Word, the baptizer is not the Spirit. The baptizer is either Christ or His disciples, His believers. Why then do we say that the Spirit has the function of baptizing?

Matthew 28:19 reveals that we need to baptize the nations into the Triune God, and the Triune God is consummated in the Spirit. The Father is the source, the Son is the course, and the Spirit is the consummation. When we have the Spirit as the consummation, we have the Father as the source and the Son as the course. If we have the Spirit, we have the Son and the Father. To be baptized into the Triune God is to be baptized into the Spirit as the consummation of the Triune God (1 Cor. 12:13).

The One whom we baptize people into is more important than the one who baptized them. The One into whom we are baptized is so important because in baptism we are mingled with Him. To be baptized into the Spirit means that the Spirit mingles us with Himself. When the Spirit puts us into Himself, we are brought into an organic union with the Triune God. This organic union with the Triune God is not accomplished by the baptizer but by the very element into which we have been baptized.

When we go out to preach the gospel, we baptize people into the Triune God, who has the Spirit as His consummation. Through this baptism, the Spirit mingles the baptized one with Him. This creates an organic union. In baptism, the baptized one is mingled with the Triune God. When we say that the Spirit has the function of baptizing, this is what we mean.

Brooding for Ministering

The Spirit also has the function of brooding for ministering

(Matt. 3:16b; Luke 3:22; John 1:32). In Genesis 1:2 the brooding of the Spirit is for the producing of life. In the New Testament, the dove came down to Jesus and brooded over Him for His ministry. These two instances of the brooding of the Spirit show that the ministry of Jesus was for producing life. The ministering of Christ is to produce life. After this brooding, Jesus began to minister, and His ministry was always to produce life, to dispense life to all His contacts.

Leading

After the brooding of the Spirit is the leading of the Spirit (Matt. 4:1; Luke 4:1b). The leading of the Spirit in the Gospels is in reference to Jesus. First, the Spirit broods over Jesus for His ministry of producing life. Then the same Spirit, the brooding Spirit, became the leading Spirit. He led Jesus to carry out His ministry for producing life.

Speaking in the Believers

The Spirit has the function of speaking in the believers (Matt. 10:20; Mark 13:11; Luke 12:12). It is hard to find a verse in the New Testament which says that the Spirit speaks in Jesus. This is because Jesus is absolutely one with the Spirit. Therefore, every time He spoke, the Spirit spoke.

With us it is a little different. First Corinthians 6:17 does say that we have been joined to the Lord and that we are one spirit with Him. We should arrive at the point that whatever we do is God's doing. God's chosen people through Christ and in the Spirit can arrive at this destination, the destination where they are one with God. Paul said that to him to live was Christ (Phil. 1:21a). This is the same as saying, "For me to live is God." Christ is God, and we are the sons of God. It is the function and work of the Spirit to make us one with God.

Because we are joined to Christ, we are the parts of Christ, the members of Christ (1 Cor. 12:12; Rom. 12:4-5; Eph. 5:30). The church is the corporate Christ, the Body-Christ. In 1 Corinthians 12:12, Paul said, "For even as the body is one and has many members, but all the members of the body being many are one body, so also is Christ." This verse refers to the corporate Christ, the Body-Christ, including all of us.

In this sense, we are all parts of Christ. Our experience of being the parts of Christ in our daily life, however, may be different. If we live by ourselves, we are not parts of Christ in our daily life.

As long as we live by the Spirit, we have the presence of the Lord. The presence of the Lord in Matthew 10:20 is the Spirit for speaking. In this portion of the Word, the Lord Jesus was instructing His disciples concerning the way to meet persecution. We should face opposition and confront attack not in ourselves, but by turning to our spirit where the Spirit of God dwells. We need to trust in Him, let Him lead us, and let Him do the speaking.

Announcing

Matthew 12:18 reveals that the Spirit is the announcing Spirit. To announce is to preach, and to preach is to proclaim or report. Although preaching, proclaiming, announcing, and reporting are synonyms, they are still a little different. When we report something, this is usually not done with a loud voice. But announcing is done loudly. Sometimes Christ preached in the way of reporting, and other times He announced. Matthew 12:18 says, "Behold, My Servant whom I have chosen, My Beloved in whom My soul delights; I will put My Spirit upon Him, and He shall announce judgment to the nations."

Casting Out Demons

The Spirit has the function of casting out demons. In Matthew 12:28 the Lord said that He cast out demons by the Spirit of God. In Luke 11:20 He said that He cast out demons by the finger of God. This means that the Spirit is signified by the finger of God. This also shows how powerful God is. Note 20[1] on this verse in the Recovery Version points out that this is a Hebraistic expression. This kind of expression means that God needs only a little strength to carry things out. To cast out demons does not need the hand of God or the arm of God; just the finger of God is powerful enough to do it. The Lord uses His arm to carry out things (Isa. 53:1; Luke 1:51a). In John 10:28 and 29, the Lord said that no one can snatch

His sheep out of His hand or out of His Father's hand. Therefore, we have two hands holding us. But to cast out demons, God needs only to use His finger, which signifies the Spirit of God.

Infilling as the Oil in the Vessel

The Spirit has the function of infilling as the oil in the vessel (Matt. 25:4, 8-9). We are likened to vessels, and the filling One is likened to oil. Oil is a symbol of the Spirit in the parable of the virgins in Matthew 25. In order to be wise virgins, we need to buy the oil. This means that we need to pay the price to gain the fullness of the Spirit.

Thrusting

Mark 1:12 says that the Spirit thrusted Jesus into the wilderness. To thrust is to drive or to impel. The Spirit drove and impelled Christ to carry out His ministry. Many times the Spirit pushes and impels us to do things. I have had the feeling often that the Spirit was urging, impelling, thrusting, and driving me. Even the Lord Jesus needed the thrusting of the Spirit. We need the Spirit's thrusting even more.

Filling Outwardly

The Spirit has the function of filling outwardly (Luke 1:15b, 41b, 67). The Greek word *pletho* refers to the outward filling of the Holy Spirit. When the Spirit fills us inwardly as the oil in the vessel, He is the essential Spirit. When He fills us outwardly, He is the economical Spirit. The infilling is for the essence of life, and the outward filling is for the work.

Overshadowing

According to Luke 1:35, the Spirit has the function of overshadowing. Overshadowing is very close to brooding. To overshadow is to cover and protect. Brooding is not for protection or covering but for producing life. In Luke 1:36 the angel said to Mary, "The Holy Spirit will come upon you, and the power of the Most High will overshadow you." When the Spirit came to Mary, He did the begetting within her; outwardly, He overshadowed her. The Spirit came to Mary inwardly to produce life, to beget, and He came to Mary outwardly to overshadow, cover, and protect her. This shows that when the Lord Jesus was begotten in Mary, Mary had the Spirit within as the essential Spirit to beget, and she had the Spirit without as the economical Spirit to overshadow her, to cover her.

Prophesying

Prophesying is another function of the Spirit. In Luke 1:67 and 2:27-29 prophesying is used mainly in the sense of speaking for God and speaking forth God. In the New Testament usage, to prophesy is mainly to speak for the Lord. With prophesying there may also be some prediction.

Communicating—Revealing

The Spirit has the function of communicating, revealing. Luke 2:25-26 says, "And behold, there was a man in Jerusalem whose name was Simeon; and this man was righteous and devout, looking for the consolation of Israel; and the Holy Spirit was upon him. And it was communicated to him by the Holy Spirit that he would not see death before he should see the Lord's Christ." Something was communicated to Simeon by the Holy Spirit. This means that something was revealed to him.

Infilling

The Spirit is also for infilling. Luke 4:1 says that Jesus was "full of the Holy Spirit." The Greek word for "full" here is the adjective *pleres*. To be full of the Spirit is the result and condition of being filled within.

Empowering

The Spirit is the empowering Spirit (Luke 4:14a; 11:20; 24:49). He is the power for preaching and for casting out demons. In Luke 24:49, the Lord told the disciples, "Stay in the city until you are clothed with power from on high." The power from on high is the Holy Spirit.

Anointing

Luke 4:18a says, "The Spirit of the Lord is upon Me, because He has anointed Me..." This verse shows that the Spirit has the function of anointing. Before the Spirit of God descended and came upon Jesus for His anointing (Matt. 3:16), He was already born of the Spirit (Luke 1:35), proving that He already had the Spirit of God within Him. That was for His birth. For His ministry, the Spirit of God descended upon Him. This was the fulfillment of Isaiah 61:1; 42:1; and Psalm 45:7 to anoint the new King and introduce Him to His people.

Feeding

The Spirit has the function of feeding. Luke 11:11-13 says, "But what father among you, whose son asks for a fish, will instead of a fish hand him a snake? Or if also he asks for an egg, will hand him a scorpion? If you then, being evil, know how to give good gifts to your children, how much more shall the Father who is from heaven give the Holy Spirit to those who ask Him?" Here the life supply is indicated by the fish, the egg, and the Holy Spirit. In verse 5 it is indicated by the loaves of bread. The Holy Spirit is the totality of the loaves, the fish, and the egg. The Spirit brings the bread, the fish, and the egg to us. He is feeding us.

Seeking as a Fine Woman

In Luke 15 there is a parable of a woman seeking a lost coin (vv. 8-10). That woman signifies the Spirit as the seeking One, who seeks the sinner as a woman seeks carefully for one lost coin until she finds it. The Spirit does some fine seeking to seek out the sinners and bring them back to God.

Regenerating

John 3 reveals the function of the Spirit in regenerating us (vv. 5-6, 8). Titus 3:5 speaks of the washing of regeneration and renewing of the Holy Spirit. In this verse the word *regeneration* is different from that for born again. It refers to a change from one state of things to another. To be born again is the beginning of this change. The washing of regeneration begins with our being born again and continues with the renewing of the Holy Spirit as the process of God's creation to make us a new man.

Speaking the Words of God

John 3:34 says, "For He whom God has sent speaks the words of God, for He gives the Spirit not by measure." Jesus, the Son of God, is the One whom the Father sent. As God's sent One, He speaks the words of God. He speaks for God, and He gives the Spirit to us without measure. This indicates that the Lord's speaking gives us the Spirit, that is, the Lord gives us the Spirit by speaking the words of God. The more we speak the words of God, the more of the Spirit we minister to others. Speaking the words of God is a sign that we have the Spirit to give to others. This corresponds with John 7:38-39, which indicates that the Spirit flows out of the believers as rivers of living water through their speaking of the Lord's words. This is also fully proven in our meetings. If we do not prophesy, we quench the Spirit. The more we speak, the more the Spirit flows out. When we speak, the Spirit is with our speaking and flows out of us to supply others. How can we minister the Spirit to others? We need to speak the word of God.

Life-giving

John 6:63 says that it is the Spirit who gives life and the flesh profits nothing. The Lord explained in this verse that what He would give people to eat was not His physical body. This is the flesh which profits nothing. What He would give is the Spirit who gives life, who is Himself in resurrection. The Lord as the Spirit in resurrection has the function of life-giving.

Flowing as Rivers

When the Lord spoke concerning the Spirit in John 7:38-39, He said that the Spirit would flow out of our innermost being as rivers of living water. The Spirit flows out of us as many rivers such as a river of patience, a river of holiness, a river of power, and a river of love. The one Spirit has many rivers, just as the one river in Genesis 2 was parted into four rivers.

Taking Care of the Saints as a Comforter, a Helper, an Intercessor, a Counselor, and an Advocate

The Spirit functions to take care of the saints as a Comforter, a Helper, an Intercessor, a Counselor, and an Advocate (John 14:16; 15:26a; 16:7). The Greek word *paracletos,* anglicized as *paraclete,* refers to one alongside who takes care of our cause, our affairs. This word may be translated as comforter, helper, intercessor, counselor, and advocate. An advocate is one who takes care of legal cases like an attorney. The Lord is like an attorney who takes care of us and our case in a very careful, detailed way.

The Lord Jesus was the first Comforter. When He was about to die, He told the disciples that He would ask the Father to send another Comforter. Actually this Comforter would be the first Comforter in a different form. When the Lord Jesus was in the flesh, He was the first Comforter; today as the life-giving Spirit, He is the second Comforter.

Making God, Christ, and the Divine Things concerning God and Christ Real

The second Comforter is the Spirit of truth, the Spirit of reality. The Spirit of reality functions to make God, Christ, and the divine things concerning God and Christ real (John 14:17a; 15:26b; 16:13a). The Spirit makes God real, makes Christ real, and makes all the divine things concerning God and Christ real. He is the reality of God, the reality of Christ, and the reality of all the divine things. The reality of sanctification, for example, is the Spirit. The reality of all the divine things, such as transformation and conformation, is the Spirit.

Indwelling

Another function of the Spirit is to dwell in us (John

14:17b). As we pointed out in the previous message, it is not an easy thing to dwell with someone day in and day out. But the Spirit has the ability to indwell us, to be with us all the time.

Teaching by Reminding

In John 14:26, the Lord said, "But the Comforter, the Holy Spirit, whom the Father will send in My name, He will teach you all things, and remind you of all things which I said to you." At the time the Lord spoke this word, He had already spoken many things to the disciples. Without the reminding Spirit, the disciples could have forgotten what He had said to them. The Spirit not only teaches us but also teaches us by reminding us of what He has spoken. He even reminds us of the things He spoke to us years ago. He teaches us by reminding us.

Witnessing

Teaching and reminding are both a kind of witnessing. John 15:26c says that the Spirit will testify of Jesus. This is His witnessing.

Convicting

The Spirit also functions to convict the world. John 16:8 says, "And having come, He will convict the world concerning sin, and concerning righteousness, and concerning judgment." At the time of our salvation, we were convicted by the Spirit of our sins, our failures, our rottenness, and our corruption. After that time, the Spirit continues to convict us. We are convicted of our wrongdoings and our bad attitudes. The Spirit within us is always doing a convicting work.

Guiding into the Truth

John 16:13 says, "But when He, the Spirit of reality, comes, He will guide you into all the reality." The Spirit leads us into all reality, or truth. The work of the Spirit is to convict the world, and then, as the Spirit of reality, to guide the believers into all the reality. This is to make all that the Son is and has real to the believers.

Disclosing the Riches of Christ
and the Things to Come

The Spirit discloses the riches of Christ and the things to come. In John 16:13b through 15 the Lord told us that all that the Father has becomes His. What God is, which is included in what God has, becomes the Lord's riches. These riches are passed on to the Spirit. Then the Spirit discloses all these riches to the disciples. Disclosing means unveiling. The Spirit unveils the riches of Christ, which Christ received from the Father. The riches of the Triune God are received by the Spirit, and the Spirit discloses them to us.

He also discloses to us the things to come. The things to come are mainly revealed in the book of Revelation. In the book of Revelation, there is a full unveiling of the coming things. Revelation shows us the first four seals of God's economy which consist of four horses with their riders (Rev. 6:1-8). These four horses with their riders signify the gospel, war, famine, and death. All these will continue until the end of this age. Then the Lord will judge the world and set up His kingdom, which will be His thousand-year reign. Eventually, there will be a new heaven and a new earth with the New Jerusalem. We will be there as parts of the New Jerusalem. These are some of the things to come. We may know these things, but we need to trust in the Spirit to give us a living unveiling to see them.

Glorifying Christ

In John 16:14a, the Lord said that the Spirit functions to glorify Him. To glorify Christ is to express Christ in His divinity as a splendor. Christ is so rich in His divinity, but His divine riches are hidden and concealed without the function of the Spirit to glorify Him. The Spirit expresses the divinity of Christ as a splendor. Glory is the divine substance of Christ expressed as a splendor. To glorify Christ is what Paul meant when he expressed his desire to magnify Christ (Phil. 1:20). To magnify Christ is to glorify Christ, to express the hidden, concealed Christ in His divinity splendidly. To express Him in His divinity as a splendor in our lives is to glorify Him.

Breathing

The Spirit was breathed into the believers by the Son in resurrection. "He breathed into them and said to them, Receive the Holy Spirit" (John 20:22). The Holy Spirit here is actually the resurrected Christ Himself because this Spirit is His breath. The Holy Spirit is thus the breath of the Son. The Greek word for Spirit in this verse is *pneuma,* a word that is used for breath, spirit, and wind. Therefore, this verse can be interpreted, "Receive the holy breath." On the day of His resurrection, the Lord Jesus breathed Himself into His disciples as the holy breath. The essential, infilling Spirit is our breath for our breathing.

CHAPTER SEVEN

THE FUNCTIONS OF THE SPIRIT

(3)

Scripture Reading: Acts 1:5; 8:15-19; 10:44, 47; 11:15-16; 19:2, 6; 2:4a; 4:8, 31; 9:17c; 13:9; 6:3, 5a; 7:55; 11:24; 13:52

IN THE NEW TESTAMENT—THE ACTS

In the previous messages, we have covered the functions of the Spirit in the Old Testament and in the four Gospels. The functions of the Spirit are what the Spirit did, what the Spirit does, and what the Spirit is going to do. In this message we want to see the functions of the Spirit in the book of Acts.

Giving Command of the Lord to the Apostles

Concerning the Lord Jesus, Acts 1:2 says, "Until the day in which He was taken up, having given command through the Holy Spirit to the apostles whom He chose." The Lord gave the command to the apostles through the Holy Spirit. The Spirit is the reality of the Lord's resurrection. Actually, the Spirit is the resurrection. When the Lord was giving command to His disciples in His resurrection, that means He was doing something in the Spirit. Actually, by that time, as the resurrected Christ, He was the Spirit. The resurrected Christ is the pneumatic Christ. Because He is the *pneuma*. He is pneumatic. The pneumatic Christ is the pneuma, and the pneuma is the Spirit as the breath. The Spirit as the breath is for breathing.

Whenever the Lord speaks, that is His breathing. John 3:34 shows that Christ is the unlimited One who speaks the words of God and who gives the Spirit without measure. Speaking the word of God is related to the giving of the Spirit. The Lord gives us the Spirit by His speaking. Christ's speaking the word of God is His breathing, and His breath is the Spirit. The Spirit as the breath is the pneumatic Christ Himself.

Without the breathing of the Spirit, our meetings would be empty. This breathing implies the speaking of the word of God. We minister the Spirit to others by our speaking of the word of God. If our speaking is normal and proper, our speaking is a part of the Lord's speaking. This speaking is a breathing out of the Spirit. After listening to such speaking, we are enlivened and full of joy. The proper speaking of the holy Word is a kind of breathing that releases the Spirit into the listeners.

Baptizing

The Spirit also has a function in the baptizing of the believers (Acts 1:5; 8:15-19; 10:44, 47; 11:15-16; 19:2, 6). When we say this, we do not mean that the Holy Spirit is the baptizing Spirit. What we mean is that the Holy Spirit is for baptizing. This is like saying that gasoline has a function in the driving of a car. Gasoline is the means and the power by which a car is driven, so the gasoline is for driving the car. The Holy Spirit is the means by which the Lord Jesus as the Head baptized all of us into one Body. Because the Spirit is the very means by which the Lord Jesus baptizes, we can say that this Spirit has the function of baptizing.

Giving the Power of God to the Apostles

In Acts 1:8 the Lord told the apostles, "But you shall receive power when the Holy Spirit has come upon you, and you shall be My witnesses both in Jerusalem, and in all Judea and Samaria, and unto the remotest part of the earth." The Holy Spirit functions in giving the power of God to the apostles. Actually, this power, the power from on high (Luke 24:49), is the Holy Spirit. The Holy Spirit has the function of being power to us.

Prophesying

The book of Acts shows that the Spirit functions in prophesying (1:16; 2:17-18; 4:25; 11:28; 19:6b; 21:11; 28:25). The Bible does tell us that the Spirit speaks, but it is hard to find a verse which directly tells us that the Spirit prophesies. This is because prophesying implies the principle of incarnation. In the principle of incarnation, God does not do anything by Himself. He does everything with man, through man, and in man. In the principle of incarnation. God cannot prophesy without man. If God speaks by Himself or if we speak by ourselves, that is not prophesying. Prophesying is our speaking with the Spirit, in the Spirit, and through the Spirit. We cannot prophesy without the Spirit, and the Spirit cannot prophesy without us. Prophesying is carried out entirely in the principle of incarnation.

Filling Outwardly

The Spirit also has the function of filling outwardly (Acts 2:4a; 4:8, 31; 9:17c; 13:9). When someone is baptized in water, he is filled with the water outwardly. To drink water is to be filled inwardly with water, whereas to be baptized is to be filled outwardly with water. In Greek, *pleroo* is used for the inward filling for life, and *pletho* is used for the outward filling for power and authority in the work. Acts 2:4 says that on the day of Pentecost, the disciples were filled outwardly with the Spirit. The wind which filled the house where they were sitting, filled it inwardly (v. 2), whereas they were filled outwardly with the Spirit. The baptistry is filled inwardly with water, but the baptized ones are filled with the water outwardly. To the baptistry, it is an inward filling. To the baptized ones, it is an outward filling.

Giving the Utterance of Tongues

In the book of Acts, the Spirit gave the utterance of tongues (2:4b; 19:6b). There are three different categories of tongue-speaking. The first one is the genuine tongue-speaking by the Holy Spirit through a believer. The second one is the tongue-speaking by a pagan with a devilish spirit.

Tongue-speaking was a Gentile phenomenon in the ancient Han dynasty of China. In Africa, there has been tongue-speaking by the pagan priests and priestesses in their idol worship. This is why Paul refers to the discerning of spirits (1 Cor. 12:10; 1 Tim. 4:1). We have to distinguish the Spirit that is of God from those that are not of God (1 John 4:1-3). The third kind of tongue-speaking is humanly manufactured. Most of the so-called speaking in tongues in the Pentecostal movement is humanly manufactured speaking. The speaking in tongues on the day of Pentecost, however, was the speaking of genuine dialects (Acts 2:4, 6, 8). The disciples were Galileans (v. 7), yet they spoke the different foreign dialects of the attendants who came from various parts of the world. This is strong proof that tongue-speaking must be an understandable language, not merely a voice or a sound uttered by the tongue.

In 1 Corinthians 14 Paul strongly belittled the gift of tongues and exalted the gift of prophecy, because his main concern was the church, not the individual believers. Speaking in tongues, even if it is genuine and proper, only edifies the speaker himself, but prophesying builds up the church. We have seen already that when we speak the word of God, the Spirit is dispensed. The safest way to minister the Spirit is to speak the word of God.

Being Poured Out upon All Flesh

Joel prophesied concerning the Spirit being poured out upon all flesh (2:28-29), and this prophecy was fulfilled on the day of Pentecost and in the house of Cornelius (Acts 2:17-18, 33; 10:45b). The fulfillment of this prophecy in Joel is the baptism in the Spirit. The outpouring of the Spirit prophesied by Joel in the Old Testament is the New Testament baptism in the Spirit, exercised by Christ the Head to put all His members into one Body. The Spirit was outpoured, and the believers in Christ were baptized in the Spirit.

We need to experience the baptism in the Spirit that has already been accomplished on the Body. In the course of my ministry, I have had a number of miraculous experiences of the outpoured Spirit. Miraculous happenings may accompany our experience of the baptism in the Spirit, but we should not seek after these things. Otherwise, we can be deceived. If these things are needed, God will perform them. But we should not seek these things. We should seek Christ Himself in the holy Word which He has given us. This is safe.

Being a Gift to the Believers

The Spirit functions as a gift to the believers (Acts 2:38; 10:45b; 15:8). It is a hard and tiring job to be with someone all the time, but the Spirit has the function of being with us always. The Spirit which is with us is a gift, a present, to us. The Spirit is a present given by God to us to be with us. The Spirit given to us by God is a living gift who is able to be with us livingly all the time. No matter where we are or what kind of situation we are in, we believers have the feeling that someone is with us. This person is the Spirit as a gift to us. His presence with us is especially striking in our times of trouble. When we are in trouble or are lonely because we are away from our loved ones, we have the deep sensation that someone is with us. This person is the Spirit as a great gift to us.

Living as God with the Church

The Spirit lives as God with the church (Acts 5:3-4, 9). In Acts 5, Ananias and Sapphira lied both to Peter and to the church, but Peter told them that they lied to the Holy Spirit. Peter also said that they did not lie to men but to God. To lie to the Spirit is to lie to God. This means that the Spirit as the very God is with the church. The Spirit with us is the presence of God. In the Old Testament, God's presence with Israel was in the form of a cloud. The cloud was God's presence, typifying the Spirit as the presence of God. When the Spirit is with us, God is with us. The Spirit is God's presence.

Co-witnessing with the Apostles

The Spirit co-witnesses with the apostles. In Acts 5:32, the apostles said, "And we are witnesses of these things, and the Holy Spirit also, whom God has given to those who obey Him." When the apostles were testifying, witnessing, the

Spirit went along with them. He co-witnessed with them. This is one of the functions of the Spirit.

Infilling

The Spirit has the function of infilling (Acts 6:3, 5a; 7:55; 11:24; 13:52). We should experience the infilling of the Spirit constantly and unceasingly. When we feel empty inwardly, this means we are short of the infilling Spirit. Something is wrong within us that is occupying us. Then we need to confess our sins, wrongdoings, shortcomings, and mistakes to the Lord so that we can experience the infilling of the Spirit.

Speaking

The Spirit also functions in speaking. Acts 6:10 says concerning Stephen, "And they were not able to withstand the wisdom and the Spirit with which he spoke." When Stephen spoke, he spoke with the Spirit. The most effective and common function of the Spirit is the Spirit's speaking. The Spirit is speaking all the time to us.

Struggling

The Spirit also has the function of struggling (Acts 7:51). This means that we may be fighting and offending the Spirit. Therefore, He struggles with us. There is a struggle between us and the Spirit.

Directing

The Spirit is also the directing Spirit (Acts 8:29; 10:19; 11:12a; 21:4). He tells us what to do and directs us.

Catching Away

After Philip finished the work of preaching, the Spirit came and caught him away (Acts 8:39a). Sometimes after we have accomplished something for the Lord, we want to enjoy the result of our work. Philip did a wonderful work of preaching, and he may have desired to enjoy the result of his work. Then the Spirit came and caught him away.

Comforting

The Spirit also has the function of comforting. Acts 9:31 says the church was going on in "the comfort of the Holy Spirit." In the midst of suffering, the church was going on in the comfort of the Holy Spirit and enjoying the Spirit as the Comforter. The Spirit as the Comforter takes care of our case, our affairs.

Anointing

As we have seen, the Spirit has the function of anointing (Acts 10:38a). To anoint is to "paint." Every coat of paint that we apply to a certain thing adds more elements of the paint to it. The Holy Spirit anoints us, paints us, with the divine element as the paint. As we are being anointed, we get more and more of God. This anointing also teaches us in all things (1 John 2:27). By the anointing of the all-inclusive compound Spirit, we know and enjoy the Father, the Son, and the Spirit as our life and life supply.

Sending

In Acts 13 the Holy Spirit sent Barnabas and Saul (vv. 2, 4). In verse 3 Barnabas and Saul were sent by the other three brothers. But verse 4 says that they were sent out by the Spirit. This proves that the three were one with the Spirit in the Lord's move, and the Spirit honored their sending as His.

Co-deciding with the Apostles and the Elders with the Whole Church

Acts 15 tells us that the Spirit co-decided with the apostles and the elders with the whole church (vv. 22a, 28). The apostles and the elders were meeting to make a decision concerning the problem of circumcision, and the decision was made, not just by them but by them with the Spirit.

As the Holy Spirit Forbidding

In Acts 16:6 the Holy Spirit forbade Paul and his co-workers from speaking the word in Asia. They may have been trying to take a direction which would not have been so holy. Therefore, they were forbidden by the Holy Spirit. Forbidding is a part of the Holy Spirit's leading.

As the Spirit of Jesus Not Allowing

Acts 16:7 says that when Paul and his co-workers tried to go into Bithynia, "the Spirit of Jesus did not allow them." The Holy Spirit's forbidding Paul to go to the left, to Asia, and the Spirit of Jesus' not allowing him to go to the right, to Bithynia, indicate a straightforward course for him and his co-workers. Thus, they went in a direct course to Macedonia through Mysia and Troas (v. 8). The Holy Spirit forbade them and the Spirit of Jesus did not allow them. In the Spirit of Jesus there is not only the divine element of God, but also the human element of Jesus and the elements of His human living and His suffering of death. Such an all-inclusive Spirit was needed for the apostles' preaching ministry, a ministry of suffering among human beings and for human beings in the human life.

Testifying

The Spirit has the function of testifying. In Acts 20:23 the Holy Spirit solemnly testified to Paul that bonds and afflictions awaited him. The Holy Spirit's testifying was only a prophecy, a foretelling, not a charge. Hence, Paul should not have taken this as a command but as a warning.

Appointing the Overseers

A great function of the Spirit is to appoint the overseers, the elders, in all the churches. Apparently, it was the apostle's appointing. Actually, in Acts 20:28 Paul said that the Holy Spirit appointed them. Paul appointed the elders by, with, and through the Holy Spirit. What Paul did in appointing the elders was the Spirit's doing. Today whenever we appoint elders, we have to trust in the Lord, doing it in oneness with the Spirit and according to the leading of the Spirit.

CHAPTER EIGHT

THE FUNCTIONS OF THE SPIRIT

(4)

Scripture Reading: Rom. 8:2, 5b, 9, 11, 13b, 14, 16, 23, 26-27; 1 Cor. 2:4, 9-15

IN THE NEW TESTAMENT—THE EPISTLES

In message seven we saw the functions of the Spirit in the book of Acts. In this message we want to begin to see the functions of the Spirit in the Epistles. We will start with Romans and 1 Corinthians.

Being the Essence of Christ's Divinity

Romans 1:4 reveals the Spirit as the essence of Christ's divinity. This verse speaks of the Spirit of God in a particular way, in a way that is different from any other place in the Bible. Verse 3 says that Christ came out of the seed of David according to the flesh. According to the flesh, Christ was a descendant of David. Then verse 4 says that Christ was "designated the Son of God in power according to the Spirit of holiness out of the resurrection of the dead." In verses 3 and 4 "according to" is used twice in a contrasting way. According to the flesh in His humanity, Christ was out of the seed of David. But according to the Spirit of holiness, Christ was designated the Son of God out of the resurrection of the dead. As the flesh in verse 3 refers to the human essence of Christ, so the Spirit of holiness in verse 4 does not refer to the person of the Holy Spirit of God, but to the essence of Christ's divinity. In Romans the first function of the Spirit is to be the essence of Christ's divinity. Christ has two essences. The essence of the nature of Christ's humanity is flesh. Of course, in His flesh there was no sin. The essence of the nature of Christ's divinity is the Spirit of holiness. This indicates that the nature of His divinity is something holy, and holiness belongs to the Spirit. The divine essence of Christ, being God the Spirit Himself (John 4:24), is of holiness, full of the nature and quality of being holy.

Being the Law of the Divine Life

The Spirit functions as the law of the divine life. Romans 8:2 speaks of "the law of the Spirit of life." To refer to the law of the Spirit means the Spirit is the law. Every person has a life, and based upon that life he has a law. A bird flies because of the law of its life. Actually, the bird itself is the bird life and the law of the bird life. The three are one. Concerning the law of the Spirit of life, we may say that the law, the Spirit, and the life are one. Cats chase mice according to the law of the cat's life. The cat's life is a mouse-chasing life. Dogs bark according to the law of the dog's life. The dog's life is a barking life.

Our life is our law and our person. Actually, every person is a law. We are a law in the sense that we always do things according to ourselves. To rise up late is a natural law for some people; they rise up late according to what they are. A person walks and talks in a certain way because he himself is a natural law. The Spirit Himself as the processed Triune God is the law of the Spirit of life. He is a law working within us. The Spirit works in us to free us by His law of life from the law of sin and death.

Love-pouring

Romans 5:5 says, "The love of God has been poured out in our hearts through the Holy Spirit who has been given to us." The Holy Spirit is used by God to pour His love into our hearts. From the day that we first called on the Lord Jesus, the love of God has been poured into our hearts through the Holy Spirit. This means that the Spirit confirms and assures us with the love of God. Although we may be afflicted, we cannot deny the presence of God's love within us.

Conveying the Things concerning Christ

Romans 8:5 says, "For those who are according to flesh mind the things of the flesh; but those who are according to spirit, the things of the Spirit." We need to ask what the things of the Spirit are. John 16:12 through 15 shows us what they are. These verses reveal that whatever the Father is, is the Son's. The Son inherits all the riches of the Father. Then whatever the Son is, is received by the Spirit. Finally, the Spirit discloses all these things to us. Based upon John 16:12 through 15, the things of the Spirit in Romans 8:5 must be the things concerning Christ. Therefore, the Spirit has the function of conveying the things concerning Christ.

Being the Reality and Reaching of God

The Spirit functions as the reality and reaching of God (Rom. 8:9a). The Father is embodied in the Son, and the Son is realized as the Spirit. Eventually, the Father, the Son, and the Spirit are fully realized as the Spirit. The Spirit is the reality of the Triune God, and the Spirit reaches us. The reaching is the application of the Triune God. The Triune God is realized as the Spirit and applied to us as the Spirit.

Being the Reality and Person of Christ

The Spirit is the reality and person of Christ (Rom. 8:9b). Romans 8:9 speaks of the Spirit of God and the Spirit of Christ. These two terms are interchangeably used. This means that the Spirit of Christ is the Spirit of God. This Spirit is Christ's reality and Christ's person.

Resurrecting, Life-giving, and Indwelling

Romans 8:11 reveals three functions of the Spirit: resur-recting, life-giving, and indwelling. Romans 8:11 says, "But if the Spirit of Him who raised Jesus from among the dead dwells in you. He who raised Christ Jesus from among the dead will also give life to your mortal bodies through His Spirit who indwells you." The Spirit resurrects us by giving life to us, and the life-giving Spirit gives us life by indwelling us. His indwelling is for life-giving, and His life-giving carries out the resurrecting. We need these functions of the Spirit daily.

Leading the Sons of God

Romans 8:14 says, "For as many as are led by the Spirit of God, these are sons of God." The Spirit functions in the believers by leading them to live a life as sons of God. We know that we are sons of God because we are led by the Spirit. This leading is not accidental or occasional. Rather, the leading of the Spirit should be habitual, constant. Continuously in our daily living we should be led by the Spirit. If we are continually led by the Spirit, we are living as sons of God in a practical way.

Witnessing

The Spirit also has the function of witnessing. Romans 8:16 says that the Spirit witnesses with our spirit that we are the children of God. In Romans 9:1 Paul said that his conscience bore witness with him in the Holy Spirit. The Spirit is witnessing that we are the children of God. Many sisters have the experience that even while they are shopping in a department store, there is a witnessing within them reminding them that they are the children of God. Sometimes while a husband is losing his temper with his wife, there is also a witnessing—"Don't forget that you are a child of God." Nothing stops a person's temper as fast as saying amen to this kind of witnessing in his spirit. The witnessing Spirit within our spirit witnesses that we are children of God.

Being the Firstfruit (Foretaste) of God as Our Portion

Romans 8:23 speaks of the Spirit being the firstfruit (foretaste) of God as our portion. The firstfruit is the first taste, the foretaste. God is our eternal portion. He is enjoyable and tasteful. The Holy Spirit, the all-inclusive Spirit, is the firstfruit of all the riches of God for our enjoyment. What we have enjoyed and what we are still enjoying of God Himself is just a foretaste. The full taste is coming. We will enjoy the full taste of God at the redemption of our body.

Helping by Interceding with Groaning and Thought-carrying

Romans 8:26 and 27 say, "And in like manner the Spirit also joins in to help us in our weakness; for we do not know for what we should pray as is fitting, but the Spirit Himself intercedes for us with groanings which cannot be uttered; but He who searches the hearts knows what is the mind of the Spirit, because He intercedes for the saints according to God." Many times we do not know how to pray because we are so weak. But the Spirit joins in, comes in, to help us in our weakness. He helps us by interceding for us with groanings which cannot be uttered. When we have a real burden to pray yet we do not know how to utter it, spontaneously we just groan with that burden without any utterable word. This groaning apparently is our groaning, but in our groaning is the groaning of the Spirit. This becomes the best prayer within which the Spirit intercedes for us by groaning together with us.

Verse 27 speaks of the mind of the Spirit. The mind of the Spirit is His thought. The searching God knows the mind of the interceding Spirit. When we are burdened to pray but do not know how to pray, this shows our weakness. At that juncture the interceding Spirit who indwells us joins in to pray for us with groanings which cannot be uttered. This is because we do not know what to utter. The groaning of the Spirit carries His thought, His mind. Gradually, after much of this interceding, we may begin to understand the situation for which we are praying. Actually, the purpose of the Spirit's groaning is that we may be fully molded and conformed to the image of God's firstborn Son (Rom. 8:29).

Being the Reality of the Kingdom of God in Righteousness, Peace, and Joy

The Spirit is the reality of the kingdom of God in righteousness, peace, and joy. God's kingdom is a life of righteousness with ourselves, peace with others, and joy with God. To be righteous with ourselves, we must be strict in dealing with ourselves. We also must have a peaceful situation with others and remain in a rejoicing joy with God all day. This is the proper kingdom life. None of us in ourselves can live a life of righteousness, peace, and joy. This is why we need the Spirit as the reality of the kingdom of God. The Spirit of God is the reality of righteousness, peace, and joy. When we have the Spirit, we have this reality, and we are really living the life of the kingdom of God.

Empowering to Abound in Hope, Resulting in Joy and Peace through Faith

The Spirit empowers us so that we can abound in hope, resulting in joy and peace through faith (Rom. 15:13). Our human life is not full of hope. People commit suicide because they do not have any hope. Since they have no hope, they feel that there is no need for them to live. Ephesians 2 says that before we were saved, we had no hope (v. 12). Romans 15:13 says, however, that as believers we need to abound in hope. I can testify that I am full of hope that the God-ordained way of meeting and serving for the building up of the Body of Christ will be flourishing and prevailing on earth.

Sanctifying

Romans 15:16 speaks of the sanctification in the Holy Spirit. This is not the objective, positional sanctification but the subjective, dispositional sanctification. God has given His Spirit to us to sanctify us, to separate us unto God for His purpose. Thus, the Holy Spirit is moving, working, and acting within us constantly to sanctify us.

Empowering for Gospel Preaching

Romans 15:19 says that Paul fully preached the gospel of Christ in the power of the Spirit. This shows that the Spirit has the function of empowering us for the preaching of the gospel.

Loving

Romans 15:30 refers to "the love of the Spirit." As Christians we should love others, but not by our natural, human love. We should love by the divine love, the love of the Spirit. Our natural, human love is not universal. However, the Spirit works in us to give us a love for all the different members of the Lord's Body (Col. 1:4, 8).

Speaking and Preaching with Power

In 1 Corinthians 2:4, Paul said, "And my speech and my preaching were not in persuasive words of wisdom, but in demonstration of the Spirit and of power." The Spirit is the speaking Spirit. The apostle's speech and preaching were not from his mind with words of speculation, but from his spirit with the release and exhibition of the Spirit, hence, of power.

Unveiling the Things God
Prepared for the Believers

The Spirit unveils the things God prepared for the believers (1 Cor. 2:9-10a). The Spirit unveils to us all the secret, mysterious, hidden, and concealed things which God prepared for us. God reveals the deep and hidden things to us through the Spirit, for these things have not been seen by man's eyes, heard by man's ears, nor have they come up in man's heart. This means that man has no idea concerning them, no thought of them. They are altogether mysterious, hidden in God, and beyond human understanding. But God has revealed them to us through the Spirit, who searches all things, even the depths of God.

Searching the Depths of God

The Spirit searches the depths of God (1 Cor. 2:10b). To know the depths of God is to know Christ in many aspects as our eternal portion. Christ is the depth of the universe because His dimensions are the dimensions of the universe (Eph. 3:18). Only the Spirit can search the deep things of God concerning Christ. The Spirit of God explores the depths of God concerning Christ and shows them to us in our spirit for our realization and participation.

Knowing the Things of God

The Spirit knows the things of God. First Corinthians 2:11b and 12 say, "So also the things of God no one has known except the Spirit of God. Now we have received not the spirit of the world, but the Spirit which is from God, that we may know the things which have been freely given to us by God." Praise the Lord that we, those who have been born of God by His Spirit, have received the Spirit of God. Hence, we are well able to know the deep things of God which He has freely given to us for our enjoyment.

Teaching the Things of God

In 1 Corinthians 2:13 Paul said that he spoke the things of God "not in words taught by human wisdom, but in words taught by the Spirit, communicating spiritual things by spiritual things." This shows that the Spirit functions in teaching the things of God. Paul spoke the spiritual things, which are the deep things of God concerning Christ, by the spiritual things, which are the spiritual words taught by the Spirit. The Spirit teaches the believers spiritual words—the things of the Spirit of God—for spiritual communication.

Discerning and Receiving the Things of God

First Corinthians 2:14 and 15 say that a soulish man does not receive the things of the Spirit of God and that they are spiritually discerned. This indicates that the Spirit discerns and receives the things of God.

Indwelling the Believers as the Temple of God

The Spirit indwells the believers as the temple of God (1 Cor. 3:16; 6:19). We believers are not ordinary people because we are collectively and universally the temple of God. In our experience we are made the temple of God by the indwelling Spirit. When a king comes to dwell in a house, that house becomes his palace. The indwelling of the Spirit is to make us God's temple.

Washing, Sanctifying, and Justifying

The Spirit has the function of washing, sanctifying, and justifying. First Corinthians 6:11 says, "These things were some of you; but you were washed, but you were sanctified, but you were justified in the name of the Lord Jesus Christ and in the Spirit of our God." This washing, sanctifying, and justifying are inward and in life. Inwardly the Spirit works to wash, sanctify, and justify the believers in life. First, we are washed from sinful things; second, we are sanctified, separated, unto God; and third, we are justified, accepted, by God.

Joining the Believers to the Lord, Making Them One Spirit with the Lord

According to 1 Corinthians 6:17, the Spirit joins the believers to the Lord, making them one spirit with the Lord. We are one spirit with the Lord by being joined to the Lord. We were joined to the Lord, brought into an organic union with Him, through believing into Him (John 3:15-16). This union is illustrated by that of the branches with the vine (John 15:4-5). It is a matter not only of life, but in life (the divine life). Such a union with the resurrected Lord can only be in our spirit.

Speaking Together with the Saints

In 1 Corinthians 7, Paul said that he gave his opinion (vv. 25, 40). He also said, "I charge, not I but the Lord" (v. 10), and "I say, not the Lord" (v. 12). He expressed his opinion in this chapter concerning marriage life. Then he said, "But I think I also have the Spirit of God" (v. 40). Paul's speaking was the Spirit's speaking. Even when Paul expressed his opinion, the Spirit still spoke. This shows that the Spirit speaks together with the saints.

Confessing with the Believers That Jesus Is the Lord

The Spirit confesses with the believers that Jesus is Lord. First Corinthians 12:3 says that "no one can say, Lord Jesus, except in the Holy Spirit." When we call, "O Lord Jesus," this is not only us calling. We are calling and confessing with the Spirit that Jesus is the Lord. Whenever a person says, "Lord Jesus," the Spirit is there with him. This is why we have to charge people to call on the name of the Lord. The Spirit is with whoever calls on the name of the Lord, and that one is saved (Rom. 10:13).

Distributing Spiritual Gifts to the Believers and Operating in Them

First Corinthians 12 reveals that the Spirit distributes spiritual gifts to the believers and operates in them (vv. 4, 7-11). The Spirit distributes different gifts to each one of us. Then He operates within us.

Baptizing the Believers into One Body and Being a Drink to the Believers

The believers are first baptized in the Spirit into one Body. Then they drink of the one Spirit (1 Cor. 12:13). To baptize is to put someone into water, and to drink is to take in water. This shows that we need the Spirit without and within. The Spirit is the reality of the water in which we are baptized and of the water which we drink.

Being the Person of the Resurrected Christ to Give Life

According to 1 Corinthians 15:45b the Spirit is the person of the resurrected Christ to give life. In resurrection Christ became a life-giving Spirit. The life-giving Spirit moves, works, and lives in us to impart life into us.

The functions of the Spirit which we have seen thus far show us much concerning the Spirit's capacity. The Spirit's capacity is the capacity of the omnipotent divine life of the Triune God. His capacity is unlimited.

CHAPTER NINE

THE FUNCTIONS OF THE SPIRIT

(5)

Scripture Reading: 2 Cor. 1:21-22; 3:3, 6, 8, 17, 18b; 13:14; Gal. 3:14; 5:16, 18, 22, 25; Eph. 2:18; 3:16; Phil 1:19

In message eight we saw the functions of the Spirit in Romans and 1 Corinthians. In this message we want to see the functions of the Spirit in 2 Corinthians, Galatians, Ephesians, and Philippians.

Anointing, Sealing, and Pledging

The Spirit has the function of anointing, sealing, and pledging (2 Cor. 1:21-22; 5:5; Eph. 1:13-14; 4:30). We are being anointed with the Spirit as the compound ointment. Exodus 30 gives us a clear picture of the all-inclusive Spirit as the compound ointment. The very ointment with which God anoints us is the processed and consummated Triune God. Before being processed and consummated, God had only divinity. He did not have humanity, nor had He passed through the processes of His human living, His all-inclusive death, His resurrection, or His ascension. But today God has been processed and consummated to be the all-inclusive, compound Spirit typified by the compound ointment.

As we have seen in message two, the ingredients of this compound ointment typify all the elements of Christ's person and work, which are included in the compound Spirit. The oil of the ointment signifies the Spirit of God with divinity. The very Spirit with whom we have been and are being anointed has been compounded with God's divinity and Christ's humanity, human living, death, resurrection, and ascension.

The Spirit as the oil, after being compounded, has become an ointment. This divine ointment, the Spirit, is the processed and consummated Triune God.

We may not have much apprehension or realization of this Spirit in our experience. But gradually, we will enter into this apprehension and realization. We will sense that the real humanity is in this compound Spirit. The more we experience the compound Spirit, the more human we will be. The humanity of Jesus is an element of the compound Spirit. Some may want to be like angels, but it is much higher to be a man for the fulfillment of God's purpose. The angels are merely our servants (Heb. 1:14). The Man Jesus with His humanity is included in the compound Spirit with which we are being anointed.

God is anointing us with Himself as the compound ointment, the divine "paint." We need to receive coat after coat of this divine paint. This painting is the anointing. We are being painted with the all-inclusive, compound Spirit as the processed and consummated Triune God. How many "coats" of the divine paint have we received? We can realize that the Apostle Paul was anointed with many coats of the divine paint, the compound Spirit. He was being anointed by the Spirit continually. We need to take him as our pattern by enjoying this anointing, this painting, day by day.

All that God is, all that God has, all that God has accomplished, and all that God has done, is doing, and will do are compounded in this anointing ointment. Day after day this compounded Spirit is anointing us with Himself as the ointment. The longer we remain in the Lord's recovery, the more of God we will gain. We gain God by being anointed inwardly with Him. He anoints Himself, paints Himself, into our being. In this way we are mingled together with Him. Second Corinthians 1:21 and 22 say that God has anointed us, sealed us, and given the pledge of the Spirit in our hearts. The anointing is God applying Himself to us. God is painting us with Himself. I have been under this painting, this anointing, for about sixty-five years.

This anointing then becomes the sealing. To be sealed with the Spirit is to have the very processed, consummated

Triune God as a mark upon us. The mark is God Himself as the compounded, sealing Spirit. The seal of the Spirit indicates that we belong to God, that we are God's property, God's inheritance, God's asset. On the one hand, we have been sealed with the Spirit. On the other hand, this sealing of God with Himself as the compounded Spirit has not ceased. It is still going on. According to Ephesians 4:30, this sealing will last until the redemption, the transfiguration, of our body. The transfiguration of our body is the issue of the sealing of the Spirit. This sealing is going on and on within us.

This sealing is another aspect of the anointing, the painting. God's painting us with Himself puts a mark upon us, and that mark, that seal, is God Himself. Day by day, our God is still sealing us with Himself. This sealing is a kind of saturating. When a seal with ink is applied to paper, the paper is saturated with the sealing ink. Likewise, when the Spirit as the living seal is applied to us, we are also saturated with Him as the divine ink. According to Ephesians 1:13-14 and 4:30, this sealing goes on until the redemption of our body. The seal of the Holy Spirit is living and works within us to permeate and transform us with God's divine element until we are matured in God's life and eventually fully redeemed in our body.

The Greek preposition for "unto" in Ephesians 4:30 may also be translated as "for." The sealing of the Spirit is going on within us for the redemption of our body. This means that the redemption of our body is the issue of the sealing of the Spirit. The sealing of the Spirit continually increases within us until our entire being is sealed, issuing in the redemption of our body. When the sealing of the Spirit reaches our body, our body will be redeemed and we will be raptured. Our rapture is the consummate step of God's salvation in the divine life. The sealing of the Spirit and the redeeming are one. Whatever God seals, He redeems. As the sealing of the Spirit is going on within us, God's subjective redemption of our being is also going on.

With the sealing of the Spirit is the pledging of the Spirit. On the one hand, we are God's inheritance, God's possession. Therefore, God put Himself upon us as a seal. On the other hand, God is our inheritance, our possession, our property, our real estate. We know that God is our possession because we have Him as our pledge, our guarantee. The pledge is the consummated, compounded Spirit given to us as the first-fruit. Romans 8:23 mentions "the firstfruit of the Spirit." Today the pledge of the Spirit is the firstfruit, the foretaste, of the Spirit, and the full taste is coming. The full taste is guaranteed by the foretaste.

For Inscribing

Paul told the Corinthians in 2 Corinthians 3:3 that they were a letter of Christ "ministered by us, inscribed not with ink, but with the Spirit of the living God." This shows that the Spirit is for inscribing. The Spirit is not the person who inscribes, but the ink with which the apostles inscribed Christ into the believers. When we write with ink, the ink is applied to the paper and becomes one with the paper. The Spirit is the ink with which the servants of God are inscribing us. This means that the divine element is being added to our being. We are receiving more heavenly, divine ink every day.

I have the consciousness that while I am ministering to the saints, I am inscribing Christ in their hearts, and they are receiving more of the Spirit as the ink. When we receive the Spirit as the ink, all the things compounded in the Spirit—Christ's divinity, humanity, human living, death, resurrection, and ascension—are added into our being. All of these elements are compounded in the divine ink, and the divine ink as the divine element is applied to us by the servants of the Lord.

Ministering

According to 2 Corinthians 3:6 and 8, the Spirit has the function of ministering. This function is similar to the function of a waiter who ministers food to people. The Holy Spirit today is ministering the crucified, resurrected, and ascended Christ to us. He is the very food which the ministering Spirit ministers to us.

Giving Life

The ministering of Christ to us gives us life. The Spirit functions to give life. Second Corinthians 3:6b says, "The Spirit gives life." First Corinthians 15:45b says, "The last Adam became a life-giving Spirit." The last Adam is the person of the resurrected Christ to give life. The Spirit gives the divine life, the compounded Triune God as life, to us.

Being the Lord and Freeing the Believers from the Veil of the Law

Second Corinthians 3:17 says, "The Lord is the Spirit, and where the Spirit of the Lord is, there is freedom." The Spirit's function is to be the Lord and also to free us from the veil, the covering, of the law. The veil of the law is the law itself. As long as we keep the law, the law is a veil that covers us from seeing Christ. The Spirit functions to free us from the covering of the law that we may have an unveiled face to behold Christ.

Transforming

Second Corinthians 3:18 reveals that the Spirit is the transforming Spirit. The Spirit functions to free us from the covering of the law that we may have an unveiled face to look at the very Christ face-to-face so that we might be transformed into His image of glory. While the Spirit, who is the Lord Himself, is freeing us from the covering of the law to help us to have an unveiled face, He is also transforming us. The Spirit adds Himself to us, and this addition of the Spirit, through a divine and spiritual metabolism, transforms us into another form. When we were under the law, we were in our old being, an old and natural form. But the freeing Spirit adds the new element of the divine Being into our being, causing a divine metabolism within us. On the one hand, the new element of God is being added to us. On the other hand, the old element of our old being is being discharged from us. Then we are transformed into the glorious image of Christ, and this transformation is "from the Lord Spirit" (2 Cor. 3:18).

Mingling

Second Corinthians 4:13 says that we have "the same spirit of faith." This spirit is God's Spirit mingled with our spirit. Therefore, another function of the Spirit is to mingle Himself with the human spirit. The thought of the mingled spirit is very strong here and in Romans 8. When Paul tells us to walk according to the spirit in Romans 8:4, he is referring to the mingled spirit. Both Dean Alford and M. R. Vincent point out that the spirit of faith in 2 Corinthians 4:13 is the mingling of the Holy Spirit with our human spirit. The compounded, consummated Spirit of God today has the function of mingling Himself with the human spirit.

Fellowshipping, Communicating

The Spirit has the function of fellowshipping, which implies communication. Second Corinthians 13:14 says, "The grace of the Lord Jesus Christ, and the love of God, and the fellowship of the Holy Spirit be with you all." According to our experience, we do not receive the love of God first. We receive the grace of Christ; then in the grace we realize the love of God. The fellowship of the Spirit is the Spirit Himself as the transmission of the grace of the Lord with the love of God for our participation.

Perfecting

The Spirit also functions to perfect us. Paul asked the Galatians, "Are you so foolish? Having begun by the Spirit, are you now being perfected by the flesh?" (Gal. 3:3). This verse indicates that the beginning Spirit is also the perfecting Spirit. The Spirit begins our spiritual life and also perfects our spiritual life.

Doing Works of Power

In Galatians 3:5 Paul indicated that the Spirit has the function of doing works of power.

Being the Blessing of the Gospel to the Nations

Galatians 3:14 says, "In order that the blessing of Abraham

might come to the nations in Jesus Christ, that we might receive the promise of the Spirit through faith." This verse reveals that the Spirit is the blessing of the gospel to the nations. Galatians 3 talks about God's blessing through Christ to all the nations. This was a promise to Abraham, and this promise was the glad tidings, the gospel, God preached to Abraham. Actually, it was the promise God gave to Abraham, but Paul considered that promise as the gospel. God promised Abraham that through one of his descendants, all the nations would be blessed. According to Galatians 3, the blessing of that promise, the blessing of the gospel God preached to Abraham, is just the all-inclusive Spirit. The all-inclusive Spirit is the very realization of Christ, who is the embodiment of the Triune God as the blessing to all the nations. We have to realize that in the gospel, the main blessing, the central blessing, we have received is this all-inclusive Spirit.

Crying, "Abba, Father"

The Spirit also has the function of crying, "Abba, Father" (Gal. 4:6). On the one hand, we are crying, "Abba, Father" (Rom. 8:15), but actually, the Spirit of God's Son is crying in our hearts.

Regenerating

John 3 tells us that we need to be reborn, to be born of the Spirit (vv. 5-6). Galatians 4:29 refers to being "born according to Spirit." We are children according to the Spirit. Such a word indicates that the Spirit is the regenerating Spirit. We all were regenerated by Him, so we became children according to Him.

Hope-expecting

According to Galatians 5:5, the Spirit is the hope-expecting Spirit: "For we by the Spirit by faith eagerly expect the hope of righteousness." Christ's coming is our hope. We should eagerly expect Him as the hope of righteousness. The Spirit always earnestly expects this hope. When we walk according to the indwelling Spirit, we spontaneously expect the coming Lord Jesus as our hope. The indwelling Spirit has a hope-expecting function.

Walking with the Believers

The believers walk by the Spirit (Gal. 5:16, 25b). This means that the Spirit is walking with the believers. We are walking by the Spirit, and the Spirit is walking with us.

Fighting against the Flesh

While the Spirit is walking with us, He is fighting against the flesh (Gal. 5:17). We have a major enemy—our flesh. Who can deal with such a major enemy? Only the Spirit can deal with our flesh. The Spirit is the fighting Spirit, fighting against our flesh. He is both the fighter and the sword, the weapon for slaying (Eph. 6:17-18).

Leading the Believers

While the Spirit is walking with us and fighting for us, He is leading us (Gal. 5:18). He will never lead us to the theater, but He will always lead us to the meetings. We get to the meetings by the leading of the Spirit. We can sense the leading of the Spirit by the inward peace. When we come to the meetings, we have peace. If we went to the movies, we would not have peace. Not having peace means that the Spirit does not lead us that way.

Bearing the Fruit of Virtues

The Spirit also has the function of bearing the fruit of virtues (Gal. 5:22-23). The Spirit who walks with us, who fights for us, and who is leading us, helps us to bear the fruit of all kinds of human and divine virtues, such as love, joy, peace, longsuffering, kindness, goodness, faithfulness, meekness, and self-control (vv. 22-23).

Sowing

According to Galatians 6:8, we need to sow unto the Spirit. Whatever we do in our human life is a sowing, and whatever we sow, we will reap. Whether we have the positive reaping or the negative reaping depends upon our sowing. If our sowing is in the flesh, that is negative. If our sowing is in the Spirit, that is positive. God wants us to have the positive sowing all day long. This is only possible by the Spirit.

Ushering the Believers to the Father

The Spirit ushers the believers to the Father (Eph. 2:18). We have access to the Father in and by the Spirit. Therefore, the Spirit ushers us. In ourselves we do not have access to the Father. The Spirit is our access. He is our usher.

Strengthening and Empowering

In Ephesians 3:16, Paul prayed that God would strengthen us with the power of the Holy Spirit. Therefore, the Holy Spirit is the strengthening Spirit and also the empowering Spirit. His strengthening and empowering is altogether in our spirit.

Uniting

Ephesians 4:3 speaks of the oneness of the Spirit. The oneness is the result of uniting. For example, the electricity in all the lamps makes them one because the inner electricity unites them together as one. We Christians are all united together as one Body by the uniting Spirit.

Being the Essence of the Body

The Spirit functions as the essence of the Body. Ephesians 4:4 says, "One Body and one Spirit." This indicates that the Spirit is the essence of the Body. The Body of Christ is composed of all the believers, but when all the believers are not living in the Spirit, they are not the members of the Body in actuality. But if they all live in the Spirit, they are living members of the Body. The Spirit is the essence of the Body.

Slaying

According to Ephesians 6:17, the Spirit as the sword has the function of slaying. The Spirit today kills the negative things within us by slaying them. The Spirit slays our flesh and our opinion.

Supplying

The Spirit within us is the supplying Spirit. Philippians 1:19 speaks of "the bountiful supply of the Spirit of Jesus Christ." The Spirit of Jesus Christ is the very realization of the incarnated, crucified, resurrected, and ascended Christ. His very person together with His incarnation, crucifixion, resurrection, and ascension are the riches of the Spirit's supply. The Spirit supplies us with the incarnation, with the death of Christ, with the resurrection of Christ, and with the ascension of Christ.

When we are down and disappointed, the Spirit within us can supply us with ascension. If we feel dead, we can pray and the Spirit within us will supply us with resurrection. Resurrection is typified by the calamus in the compound ointment in Exodus 30. It is a reed that shoots up out of the muddy situation into the air. We need to experience the resurrection of Christ and the ascension of Christ in the Spirit. The Spirit also supplies the killing death of Christ. We may have a negative thought about a certain brother or sister, but the indwelling Spirit supplies us with the killing of Jesus to kill this thought. If we are proud, the indwelling Spirit can supply us with Jesus as our humility. This supply causes us not to seek our own glory but to give all the glory to Him. The indwelling Spirit supplies all these things within us. When Paul wrote concerning the bountiful supply of the Spirit, he was in prison. How could he endure that kind of situation? He could only endure it by the inner supply, the bountiful supply, of the Spirit of Jesus Christ. Thank the Lord for this wonderful, bountiful supply.

Serving

The Spirit also has the function of serving. In Philippians 3:3, Paul said that we serve by the Spirit of God. We serve as priests by the Spirit of God, not by the ordinances of the law; we boast in Christ, not in the law; and we have no confidence in the flesh, but in the Spirit.

Chapter Ten

THE FUNCTIONS OF THE SPIRIT

(6)

Scripture Reading: 1 Thes. 5:19-20; 1 Tim. 3:16; 2 Tim. 1:14; Titus 3:5b; Heb. 6:4b; 9:14; 10:29c; James 4:4-5; 1 Pet. 1:10-12a; 4:14; 1 John 3:24; 4:13, 6; 5:6-9; Rev. 2:7; 14:12-13; 22:17

In this message we want to continue to see the functions of the Spirit in the Epistles of the New Testament.

Preaching in the Gospel

The Spirit has the function of preaching in the gospel. When we preach the gospel, the Spirit preaches in our preaching (1 Thes. 1:5; 1 Pet. l:12b).

Giving Joy to the Believers in Affliction

Another function of the Spirit is to give us joy in our affliction (1 Thes. 1:6b). When we are suffering, we enjoy the Spirit's joy.

Inspiring for Prophecies

The Spirit has the function of inspiring for prophecies. First Thessalonians 5:19 and 20 say, "Do not quench the Spirit. Do not despise prophecies." The Spirit is quenched by us when we would not speak. We all have to admit that we quench the Spirit many times. In the meetings of the church, we may have the feeling that we should stand up to speak, but we do not speak. We have to be strong in making up our mind to speak.

We Christians have a very wonderful function. When we speak, the Spirit comes out. In 2 Thessalonians 3:1, Paul asked the saints to pray for him that the word of the Lord might run and be glorified. For the word of the Lord to run is for the word of the Lord to have free course (see 2 Thes. 3:1—KJV). The free course of the word is our speaking. If no one spoke the word of God, this would mean that God's word was fully blockaded. If we are going to let the word of God run, we have to speak. We should not despise prophecies. That means we should not despise the speaking. The prophecies mentioned in 1 Thessalonians 5 are those described in 1 Corinthians 14. Verse 19 of 1 Thessalonians 5 tells us not to quench the Spirit. Then verse 20 tells us not to despise prophecies. These two things go together. If we quench the Spirit, we surely despise prophecies.

First Thessalonians 5:19 and 20 imply the inspiring of the Spirit in speaking. We should speak whether we feel it is the right time or the wrong time to speak (2 Tim. 4:2). Actually, the time is always right for us to speak. The considerations in our mind that discourage us from speaking for the Lord are devilish. We need to reject such considerations. We may have a burden to speak and yet not know how to begin our speaking. I have learned not to consider what I would speak as an opening word. We just need to stand and speak. Quite often when I begin to speak, I am not very clear what I am going to speak. But the Lord is faithful to give me the living speaking by the Spirit. Of course, this does not mean that we should speak in a loose or nonsensical way. We need to look to the Lord as the Spirit, trusting Him to speak in our speaking. Still, as long as we speak, this is better than not speaking.

We should not be overly concerned about making mistakes when we speak. When we do things in a wrong way, we learn to do them in the right way. If a person wants to learn how to play the piano, he must practice and make mistakes to learn how to play correctly. His tutor will correct him. Our tutor in our speaking for the Lord is the Spirit. If we speak wrongly in a meeting, the Spirit within us will adjust us. For us to speak is to give the word of God a free course.

Vindicating Christ,
Who Was Manifested in the Flesh

According to 1 Timothy 3:16, the Spirit functioned to vindicate Christ, who was manifested in the flesh. The incarnated Christ in His human living was not only vindicated as the Son of God by the Spirit (Matt. 3:16-17; Rom. 1:3-4), but also justified, proved, and approved as right and righteous by the Spirit (Matt. 3:15-16; 4:1). He was manifested in the flesh, but vindicated and justified in the Spirit. He was in the flesh manifesting God, and He lived in the Spirit (Luke 4:1, 14; Matt. 12:28). This Spirit vindicated that He was God manifested in the flesh.

Speaking in Prophesying

The Spirit also functions to speak in prophesying. First Timothy 4:1 says, "The Spirit says expressly that in later times some will depart from the faith." This verse does not mean that the Spirit speaks directly without some human instrument or vessel. The Spirit speaks through the believers' prophesying. When the believers prophesy, the Spirit speaks in their prophesying.

Indwelling and Guarding
the Deposit of Truth within Us

The Spirit indwells us and guards the deposit of truth within us (2 Tim. 1:14). The Holy Spirit dwells in our spirit (Rom. 8:16). Hence, to guard the good deposit through the Holy Spirit requires us to exercise our spirit.

Renewing

Titus 3:5 speaks of the renewing of the Holy Spirit. We are receiving the new supply of the Spirit to renew us metabolically. The Holy Spirit is the divine person, washing and renewing us in the divine element to make us a new creation with the divine nature to be heirs of God in His eternal life, inheriting all the riches of the Triune God. The Spirit began to renew us from our regeneration and is renewing us continuously every day and all day to make us a new creation with the divine life.

Exhorting

Hebrews 3:7 and 8 say, "Wherefore, even as the Holy Spirit says, Today if you hear His voice, do not harden your hearts, as in the provocation, in the day of trial in the wilderness." These verses show that the Spirit also has the function of exhorting, or warning.

Being a Portion to the Believers

Hebrews 6:4 says that we are partakers of the Holy Spirit. Therefore, the Holy Spirit is a portion for us to enjoy, to partake of. At the time of our salvation, we did not partake of the Spirit once for all. This partaking of the Spirit is going on every day because the very Spirit, of whom we partake, is within us for our enjoyment.

Showing by the Types

In Hebrews 9:6-8, Paul speaks of the type of the tabernacle with the Holy Place and the Holy of Holies. Through this type the Spirit speaks something concerning the New Testament. The Spirit shows us something of the New Testament by the Old Testament types.

Being the Means through Which Christ Offered Himself to God

Hebrews 9:14 says that Christ through the eternal Spirit offered Himself to God. This shows that the Spirit was the means through which Christ offered Himself to God.

Testifying the Lord's Word

The Spirit testifies the Lord's word. Hebrews 10:15-17 shows how the Spirit speaks something to testify what the Lord has spoken already in the Bible. The Bible is the written Word. When we read it, the living Spirit within us testifies to what is written in the Bible.

Embodying the Grace of God

Hebrews 10:29c refers to the Spirit of grace. This means that God's grace is embodied in the Spirit. If you have the Spirit, you have God's grace. If you receive the Spirit, you receive grace.

Envying the Believers for God

James 4:4 and 5 show that the Spirit envies the believers for God. God and Christ are our Husband (Isa. 54:5; 2 Cor. 11:2). We should be chaste and love Him alone with our entire being (Mark 12:30). If our heart is divided by loving the world, we become adulteresses. Our God is a jealous God, and His Spirit is jealous over us with a jealousy of God (2 Cor. 11:2).

Sanctifying the Sinners for Believing in Christ

The Spirit has the function of sanctifying the sinners for believing in Christ. In 1 Peter 1:2 the sanctifying of the Spirit is not concerning those who are already believers but concerning the sinners who are going to be believers. This is the sanctification of the Spirit before our believing in Christ. The Holy Spirit's sanctification has different steps. The first step is before our repentance and believing, and the second step is after our believing to sanctify us positionally.

The woman's seeking of the lost coin in Luke 15 typifies the Spirit's seeking of the sinner (vv. 8-10). The woman lights a lamp and sweeps the house to find the lost coin. This is the Spirit's work to enlighten and expose the sinner's position and condition that he may repent and return to the Father, as the prodigal son did (vv. 17-20). (This is the first step of the Holy Spirit's sanctification.) Once he returns to the Father and receives Christ, the Spirit then takes another step to sanctify him dispositionally.

As the Spirit of Christ
Witnessing Beforehand the Death
and Glorification of Christ as a Revelation
to the Old Testament Prophets

In 1 Peter 1:10-12a we see the Spirit as the Spirit of Christ witnessing beforehand the death and glorification of Christ as a revelation to the Old Testament prophets. These verses show that the Spirit of Christ was there already in the Old Testament. When the Old Testament prophets were prophesying concerning Christ, the Spirit of Christ was in them, witnessing to them how and when Christ would die and how and when Christ would be glorified, first in His resurrection and then in His ascension. We may wonder how the Spirit of Christ could have been in the Old Testament. We always consider the element of time, but with Christ, with God, there is no time element. When the prophets in the Old Testament predicted Christ's death, resurrection, and ascension, the Spirit of Christ within them was witnessing. The Spirit's witnessing means that the Spirit within them was saying, "What you are speaking now concerning the coming Christ is right." The Old Testament prophets were not merely motivated by the Holy Spirit to prophesy. While they were prophesying, the Spirit of Christ was witnessing to them.

Testifying God and the Christ of Glory on the Believers Who Are Suffering Reproach for Christ

First Peter 4:14 says that the Spirit of glory rests upon the reproached, persecuted believers. When the believers are being persecuted, being reproached, for Christ's sake, the Holy Spirit is resting upon them. This Spirit is called the Spirit of glory. Note 2 on 1 Peter 4:14 in the Recovery Version says concerning the Spirit of glory and of God: Literally, the Spirit of glory and that of God. The Spirit of glory is the Spirit of God. The Spirit of glory is the One through whom Christ was glorified in His resurrection (Rom. 1:4). This very Spirit of glory, being the Spirit of God Himself, rests upon the suffering believers in their persecution for the glorification of the resurrected and exalted Christ, who is now in glory.

Prophesying

Second Peter 1:21 says, "For no prophecy was ever borne by the will of man, but men spoke from God, being borne by the Holy Spirit." According to the context of this verse, prophesying here is predicting. This section of the Word says something concerning the Old Testament prophets' prophesying, foretelling, or predicting the things concerning Christ. No prophecy was ever carried along by the will of man. Man's will, desire, and wish, with his thought and solution, are not the source from which any prophecy came; the source is God, by whose Holy Spirit men were carried along, as a ship by the wind, to speak out the will, desire, and wish of God.

Confirming God's Abiding in Us

The Spirit also confirms that God abides in us. We know that God abides in us because of the Spirit given to us (1 John 3:24; 4:13). The Spirit is within us to confirm that God dwells in us, that God abides in us. Actually, the indwelling Spirit is God, so the Spirit confirms what God does.

Confessing That Jesus Christ Has Come in the Flesh

The Spirit has the function of confessing that Jesus Christ has come in the flesh (1 John 4:2). Whenever we say in a proper way that Jesus has come in the flesh, that indicates that we have the Holy Spirit within us. At the Apostle John's time, there was a heresy being spread that Christ was not a man. Such heresy undermines not only the Lord's incarnation but also His redemption and resurrection. Since Christ was conceived of the Spirit (Matt. 1:18) to be born in the flesh (John 1:14), the Spirit would never deny that He has come in the flesh through divine conception.

Being the Spirit of Truth

First John 4:6 says that the Spirit is the Spirit of truth. Truth means reality. The Spirit of truth is also mentioned in John 14:17; 15:26; and 16:13. The Spirit of truth is a particular divine title used by John. Neither Paul nor Peter used this title. Such a title means that the very Spirit is the reality of the doctrines concerning the Trinity. This is one of His functions. He makes all the teachings concerning Christ, concerning God, and concerning the divine Trinity real.

Being the Reality, Testifying the Things concerning Jesus Christ, the Son of God

The Spirit is the reality, testifying the things concerning Jesus Christ, the Son of God (1 John 5:6-9). Christ is a mystery. The Son of God is altogether hidden from the world. The worldly people without the Spirit cannot understand the things concerning Him. But we have the Spirit within us, and the indwelling Spirit makes everything taught concerning Christ in the New Testament so real to us.

For the Believers' Prayer

The Spirit is also for the believers' prayer (Jude 20). The Spirit functions for us to pray. We pray in the Holy Spirit. The entire blessed Trinity is employed and enjoyed by us believers in our praying in the Holy Spirit, keeping ourselves in the love of God, and awaiting the mercy of our Lord unto eternal life.

As the Seven Spirits, the Sevenfold Intensified Spirit of God, Meeting the Need of the Seven Churches, Which Signify All the Churches in the Seven Stages through the Centuries in Degradation

In the book of Revelation, the Spirit functions as the seven Spirits, the sevenfold intensified Spirit of God, meeting the need of the seven churches, which signify all the churches in the seven stages through the centuries in degradation (Rev. 1:4; 3:1; 4:5; 5:6). How could the one Spirit be seven Spirits? In typology, there is the one lampstand with seven lamps. In existence it is one lampstand, but in function it is seven lamps. The stand is one, but the lamps are seven. This signifies that the one Spirit of God has a sevenfold intensified function.

Because there are seven churches, the Spirit of God has to be sevenfold. This means He is adequate and He is altogether sufficient to meet the need of all the churches. Sevenfold means all-inclusive. The seven churches signify all the churches in the seven stages through the centuries in degradation. The sevenfold intensified Spirit of God meets the need of the degraded churches. The seven Spirits are before the throne of God for God's administration, especially in the local churches (Rev. 1:4). The throne is for government.

The seven Spirits are the means for Christ, in taking care of the local churches as the High Priest trimming the seven lamps in the Holy Place, to speak to the church in Sardis, a dying church. Revelation 3:1 speaks of "He who has the seven Spirits of God and the seven stars." This is Christ as the One who takes care of the church. He spoke to the church in Sardis, a dying church. Such a dying church needed such a Christ to make it living through the seven Spirits. This verse also implies that the seven Spirits are for the seven stars. The seven stars are the leading ones. To be a star taking the lead in the church, you need the sevenfold Spirit.

The seven Spirits function as the seven lamps of fire burning before the throne of God, executing God's administration by enlightening and burning for judging and stirring up (Rev. 4:5; Zech. 4:2, 6). Because we may be in darkness, we need the enlightening. In darkness, we are also dead, so we need the judgment to burn away all the dross. Meanwhile, we need to be motivated, stirred up. In the degraded churches, such enlightening and judging are surely needed.

The seven Spirits also function as the seven eyes of the Lamb (of Jehovah—Zech. 4:10) being sent forth into all the earth for watching over, observing, and searching all the churches with the power of Christ—the seven horns of the Lamb (Rev. 5:6). Revelation refers to the seven eyes of the Lamb, but Zechariah 4 speaks of the seven eyes of Jehovah. The seven Spirits are the seven eyes of the Lamb, of Jehovah, sent forth into all the earth. These eyes are for watching, for observing. Today we have seven eyes watching over us. We may not have this kind of realization. Instead we may be loose and light. But we have to realize that Christ is watching over us with seven eyes. He is observing us. The seven Spirits as the seven eyes of the Lamb are for observing and searching the churches with the power of Christ. The seven eyes go along with the seven horns of the Lamb. Christ's watching eyes are observing and searching with His power.

Speaking to the Churches

Chapters two and three of Revelation say seven times that the Spirit speaks to all the churches (2:7, 11, 17, 29; 3:6, 13, 22). The Spirit as the sevenfold intensified Spirit is now speaking to all the churches.

Speaking to Testify of the Labors and Works of the Martyrs

Revelation 14:12 and 13 say, "Here is the endurance of the saints, those who keep the commandments of God and the faith of Jesus. And I heard a voice out of heaven, saying, Write, Blessed are the dead who die in the Lord from this time forth. Yes, says the Spirit, that they may rest from their labors; for their works follow with them." "The dead" here refers to the martyrs under the persecution of Antichrist during the great tribulation. The Spirit functions in speaking to testify of the labors and works of the martyrs.

Speaking with the Bride as the Universal Couple to Express the Consummated Triune God in the Transformed Tripartite Man in God's Economy

The Spirit also functions in speaking with the bride as the universal couple to express the consummated Triune God in the transformed tripartite man in God's economy (Rev. 22:17). At the end of the entire Bible, the sevenfold intensified Spirit, who has been processed and consummated to be the consummation of the processed Triune God, is the Husband. He is the Husband because He speaks with the bride, the wife. The One who speaks with the bride must be the Husband. The wife is the bride and the Husband, the Spirit, is the One who is speaking with the bride. The consummated Triune God is speaking here as *the* Spirit. *The* Spirit is speaking as the Husband with His wife, the bride.

The bride of this couple is the transformed tripartite man. Such a couple is the consummation of all the work of God through the old creation and the new creation and the consummation of the entire Bible. The working God eventually becomes the consummated Triune God, and the redeemed man eventually becomes the transformed tripartite man. The consummated Triune God is the Husband, and the transformed tripartite man is the bride. This couple is altogether the completion and the consummation of God's eternal economy. We are a part of this universal bride. We are in the bride because we are a part of the bride. We are not alone because we have our Bridegroom! We are not a part of a widow. We are a part of the bride who has the Bridegroom!

Chapter Eleven

WHAT THE SPIRIT IS TO GOD AND TO CHRIST

Scripture Reading: John 4:24; Luke 1:35; Hag. 2:5; 1 John 3:24; 4:13; Rom. 8:11; 5:5; 14:17; 15:13, 30; Acts 9:31; Matt. 28:19; Rev. 22:17a; Rom. 1:4; John 14:16-20; 1 John 5;6b; John 15:26; 16:13-15; 1 John 5:6-7; 1 Cor. 15:45b; 2 Cor. 3:17-18; Rom. 8:2

In previous messages we have seen the functions of the Spirit in the New Testament. In this message we want to see what the Spirit is to God and to Christ. If we are going to experience God and Christ, we must know what the Spirit is to God and what the Spirit is to Christ.

TO GOD

The Spirit Being the Essence of God's Being

The Spirit is the essence of God's being. John 4:24 says, "God is Spirit." In the Greek text there is no article before the word *Spirit*. This is like saying that a table is wood. This indicates not only that the table is made of wood but also that the very essence of the table is wood. When we say that a ring on a person's hand is gold, we are referring to its essence. The essence is the intrinsic content of the substance. The Spirit is God's very essence. The essence of God's being, of what God is, is Spirit.

The word for Spirit in Hebrew is *ruach,* and in Greek it is *pneuma.* These words can be translated as spirit, breath, or wind. In Ezekiel 37 *ruach* is translated as Spirit, breath, and wind (vv. 5, 9, 14). In John 3 *pneuma* is translated as Spirit (v. 6) and as wind (v. 8). How these words are translated depends upon the context. According to the context of John 3:6, *pneuma* here surely refers to the Spirit—"that which is born of the Spirit is spirit." In verse 8, *pneuma* must be translated as wind because it blows and the sound of it can be heard. The very essence of the God whom we worship is *pneuma,* Spirit.

The Spirit Being God's Reaching Man, God's Abiding among Man and in Man, and God's Indwelling Man

The Spirit is God's reaching man. When God reaches us, He is the Spirit. The strongest proof of this is in Luke 1:35. The angel told Mary that the Holy Spirit would come upon her. The Holy Spirit was God's coming upon Mary. This was for the incarnation of God. The incarnation of God is just God's coming to man, God's reaching man. Every morning we need to enjoy God's reaching, God's coming to us.

The Spirit is also God's abiding among man (Hag. 2:5). This was mostly in the Old Testament. To abide is to remain. In the New Testament, God's remaining is not merely among us but mainly in us. Therefore, the New Testament uses the word *in* instead of the word *among.* In 1 John 3:24 and 4:13, we are told that God's abiding in us is by the Spirit. We know that God abides in us because the Spirit is within us. The very God abiding in us is the Spirit. The Spirit is also God's indwelling man. This is shown in Romans 8:11, which says that the Spirit of the resurrecting God indwells us.

The Spirit Being the Means of God for Him to Dispense His Attributes to Man

The Spirit is the means of God for Him to dispense His attributes to man (Rom. 5:5; 8:11; 14:17; 15:13, 30; Acts 9:31). God has many attributes such as His mercy, His grace, His love, His life, His light, His righteousness, His holiness, and His patience. The means for these attributes of God to be ours is the Spirit. Through the Spirit, we can possess and enjoy them. The many attributes of God come to us through the channel of the Spirit.

The Spirit Being
the Consummation of the Triune God

The Spirit is the consummation of the Triune God (Matt. 28:19). Eventually, God is called *the* Spirit, and the transformed tripartite man is the bride (Rev. 22:17a). The Spirit is the Bridegroom, and the bride is the transformed man. The Spirit is the consummation of the Triune God. Consummation means completion. Our God has been completed because He has been processed and compounded. We are the members of Christ, who is the embodiment of such a processed God. We possess God's life and God's nature. This makes us children of God, sons of God, and even heirs of God. We are members of the family of God, our Father. This is because we are indwelt by the Spirit, who is the consummation of the Triune God.

TO CHRIST

The Spirit Being the Essence
of Christ's Divine Being

The Spirit is the essence of Christ's divine being. In Romans 1:3-4 Paul said that Christ "came out of the seed of David according to the flesh, and was designated the Son of God in power according to the Spirit of holiness out of the resurrection of the dead." According to the flesh, Christ came out of the seed of David. But according to the Spirit of holiness, He was designated the Son of God in resurrection. The Spirit of holiness here is in contrast with Christ's flesh. As the flesh refers to the human essence of Christ, the Spirit of holiness refers to the divine essence of Christ. The Spirit of holiness is the very essence of Christ's divine person, His divine being.

The Spirit Being the Realization of Christ

John 14:16-20 presents a revelation of the Spirit as the realization of Christ. The Lord said that He would pray to the Father to give the disciples another Comforter, and this other Comforter is the Spirit of reality. Eventually, this Spirit of reality is the realization of Christ. After His resurrection, the Lord as the Spirit lives in His disciples that they may live Him (v. 19). He told the disciples that in the day of resurrection, they would know that He was in the Father, that they were in Him, and that He was in them.

In John 14:16-20 the Triune God is greatly defined. The Lord's word here covers the Father, the Son, and the Spirit in a way to help us see that the Spirit of reality is the realization of Christ. Christ the Son is the Father's embodiment, and the Spirit is the Son's realization. In other words, the Father is embodied in the Son, and the Son is realized as the Spirit.

The Spirit Being the Reality of Christ

The Spirit is the reality of Christ. The Spirit is the realization of the Son because the Spirit is the reality of the Son. First John 5:6b says, "The Spirit is the truth." The truth is the reality, and the reality is Christ. The Spirit who is the truth, the reality (John 14:16-17; 15:26), testifies that Jesus is the Son of God, in whom is the eternal life. By thus testifying, He imparts the Son of God into us to be our life (Col. 3:4).

The Spirit Being the Witness of Christ

The Spirit is the witness of Christ (John 15:26; 1 John 5:6-7). Whatever the Father is and has is the Son's, whatever the Son is and has is received by the Spirit, and the Spirit discloses to us all that He receives (John 16:13-15). This means that the Spirit is the witness of Christ. All the riches of the Triune God reach us in the Spirit. Therefore, everything of the Triune God is ours. Whenever the Spirit speaks, He speaks Christ as the embodiment of the Triune God. He speaks all of what Christ is and has. This is a kind of witnessing. The Spirit witnesses Christ.

The Spirit Being
Christ as the Life-giving Spirit

The Spirit is Christ as the life-giving Spirit (1 Cor. 15:45b). In redeeming us on the cross, He was Jesus in the flesh. But in giving life to us, He is the life-giving Spirit. As the Lamb, He redeemed us on the cross. As the life-giving Spirit, He gives us life within.

The Spirit Being Christ as the Lord—
the Lord Spirit

The Spirit is Christ as the Lord—the Lord Spirit (2 Cor. 3:17-18). The Lord Spirit may be considered a compound title like the Father God and the Lord Christ. This expression strongly proves and confirms that the Lord Christ is the Spirit and the Spirit is the Lord Christ. Christ is the Lamb, the life-giving Spirit, and eventually, the Lord Spirit.

The Spirit Being Christ as Life to Man

The Spirit is Christ as life to man (Rom. 8:2). The New Testament reveals that Christ is life (John 11:25), even our life (Col. 3:4). However, Christ can be life to us only in the reality of the Spirit. Hence, it is actually the Spirit of life who is life to God's chosen people. The Triune God as the Spirit of life makes sinners into sons of God who become the living members of the Body of Christ.

A CONCLUDING WORD

According to the New Testament revelation, the Spirit of God is the very essence of both God and Christ. This Spirit, as the essence of God and Christ, is God's reaching of man and Christ's realization to us. It is through this Spirit that we receive God. It is also by the Spirit that we realize Christ. Hence, our experience of God and of Christ is altogether a matter of this Spirit. Such a Spirit today is dwelling in our spirit. So we have to learn how to exercise our spirit that the Spirit within our spirit may be able to make God and Christ real to us for our experience and enjoyment.

CHAPTER TWELVE

THE SPIRIT AND THE CROSS

Scripture Reading: John 14:16-20; Matt. 28:19; Rom. 8:2; 2 Cor. 3:6b; John 19:34; Exo. 17:6; 1 Cor. 1:23; 2:2; Gal. 5:22-24; Phil. 3:10; 1 Cor. 1:17-18; Gal. 6:12; Heb. 9:26; 2:14; Col. 2:15; Gal. 6:14; 2:20; Rom. 6:6; Eph. 2:15; Col. 2:14; Rom. 8:13b

In the previous message, we saw what the Spirit is to God and to Christ. In this message we want to fellowship concerning the Spirit and the cross. The Spirit and the cross are both the consummation of Christ's redemptive work. Christ has completed His redemptive work, and the result of this work is the Spirit and the cross.

The Spirit after Christ's redemptive work with His death and resurrection is not the same as He was before Christ's death and resurrection. Before His death and resurrection, the Spirit was merely the Spirit of God. But afterwards the Spirit became the consummated Spirit. After Christ's redemption, the Spirit is called the Spirit of Jesus (Acts 16:7), the Spirit of Christ (Rom. 8:9), and the Spirit of Jesus Christ (Phil. 1:19). Before the death of Christ, there was the Spirit of God but not the Spirit of Jesus, the Spirit of Christ, and the Spirit of Jesus Christ.

Acts 16:6 and 7 say, "And they passed through the country of Phrygia and Galatia, having been forbidden by the Holy Spirit to speak the word in Asia. And when they had come down to Mysia, they tried to go into Bithynia, and the Spirit of Jesus did not allow them." In these verses both the Holy Spirit and the Spirit of Jesus are mentioned. The interchangeable use of the Spirit of Jesus with the Holy Spirit reveals that the Spirit of Jesus is the Holy Spirit. The Holy Spirit is a general title of the Spirit of God in the New Testament; the Spirit of

Jesus is a particular expression concerning the Spirit of God
and refers to the Spirit of the incarnated Savior who, as Jesus
in His humanity, passed through human living and death on
the cross.

We can see the particular functions of the Holy Spirit and
the Spirit of Jesus in Acts 16:6 and 7. The Holy Spirit forbade
Paul and his co-workers, and the Spirit of Jesus did not allow
them. The Holy Spirit is the sanctifying Spirit. Sanctifying
is always a matter of forbidding. The Holy Spirit's forbidding separates us, sanctifies us. The Holy Spirit's work is to
sanctify us by constantly forbidding us. If we hear the Holy
Spirit say "no" to us from morning to evening, we are blessed
because we are being sanctified. We need to hear the Holy
Spirit's "no" again and again for our sanctification.

The Spirit of Jesus either allows us or does not allow us.
To allow is to let you go. This is for accomplishing something.
The Spirit of Jesus is always sending us to accomplish something. We have to go to do the will of God just as the Man
Jesus did. Jesus was a man who was always under the cross.
In order to work for the Lord, we must be sanctified, on the
one hand, and we must be under the cross, on the other hand.
The Spirit of Jesus is the Spirit of a person who was continually under the cross. The same Spirit is the Holy Spirit and
the Spirit of Jesus. The Holy Spirit says "no" to sanctify us,
and the Spirit of Jesus says "go" to send us out to accomplish
the will of God under the cross.

The Spirit is also the Spirit of Christ and the Spirit of
Jesus Christ. The emphasis of the Spirit of Christ mentioned
in Romans 8:9 is upon the resurrection and the imparting of
life. In Philippians 1:19 Paul mentions the bountiful supply
of the Spirit of Jesus Christ. Paul spoke this when he was in
prison. He needed a bountiful supply not only of the Spirit of
Jesus but also of the Spirit of Christ, that is, of the Spirit
of Jesus Christ. The Spirit of Jesus is mainly for the Lord's
humanity, human living, and death. The Spirit of Christ is
mainly for the Lord's resurrection. The Spirit of Jesus Christ
includes both of these aspects. When Paul was in prison, he
needed the compound, all-inclusive, life-giving Spirit of the
Triune God which includes the elements of the Lord's death

and resurrection. It was by the bountiful supply of the Spirit of Jesus Christ that Paul's salvation was consummated. He said in verse 19, "For I know that for me this shall turn out to salvation through your petition and the bountiful supply of the Spirit of Jesus Christ." Paul's being sustained and strengthened to live and magnify Christ was his salvation (vv. 20-21).

The Spirit of Jesus Christ is a compound Spirit. The compound ointment in Exodus 30:23-25 was a full type of the compound Spirit of God, who is now the Spirit of Jesus Christ. This ointment was a compound of oil with four spices. The oil signifies the unique God. The four spices signify Christ's humanity, human living, and His death and resurrection. Today the Spirit of Jesus Christ is not just oil but an all-inclusive ointment. This compounded Spirit is the result, the produce, the issue, the coming out, of Christ's redemptive work.

The complete and full redemptive work of Christ began with His incarnation and was completed with His resurrection. When Christ entered into resurrection, as the last Adam, He became the life-giving Spirit (1 Cor. 15:45b). This life-giving Spirit is not merely the oil but the ointment. In this life-giving Spirit, there is incarnation, human living, the all-inclusive death, and resurrection. On the evening of Christ's resurrection, He came back to the disciples, breathed into them, and said, "Receive the Holy Spirit" (John 20:22). The Holy Spirit, the Holy Breath, is the very compounded Spirit, the consummation of Christ's redemptive work.

After the book of Acts, the New Testament covers these two basic items—the Spirit and the cross. The ultimate consummation of Christ's marvelous work in the universe is the Spirit and the cross, the all-inclusive death of Christ. Through His all-inclusive death, Christ has dealt with everything negative and has redeemed all things (Col. 1:20). In His marvelous resurrection, He became the Spirit, who is the consummation of the processed and consummated God. Such a Spirit is the positive aspect of Christ's redemptive work.

THE SPIRIT

The Spirit is the realization of Christ, who is the embodiment of the Triune God (John 14:16-20). The embodiment of the Triune God is Christ, and this Christ is realized as the Spirit. The Spirit is also the consummation of the Triune God (Matt. 28:19), the Spirit of life, and the life-giving Spirit (Rom. 8:2; 2 Cor. 3:6b). Furthermore, the consummated Spirit is the positive consummation of the work of Christ (John 19:34). Such a Spirit is the issue of the cross of Christ (John 19:34; Exo. 17:6). Just as the rock was smitten by Moses in the Old Testament to flow out water for the people to drink, Christ was smitten on the cross by the law, typified by Moses. Then the living water flowed out of Him. This living water is the Spirit as the issue of the Lord's all-inclusive death.

The Spirit of the crucified Christ is always bringing us to the cross of Christ (1 Cor. 1:23; 2:2; Gal. 5:22-24). As Christians, our destiny is to be crucified, to be crossed out. The religious Jews in Paul's day were proud of their traditional religion, and the philosophical Greeks were haughty in their worldly wisdom. In 1 Corinthians Paul said that Jews asked for signs and Greeks sought wisdom (1:22), but he preached Christ crucified (v. 23). Then he said that he determined to know only Jesus Christ and this One crucified (2:2). The Spirit of Christ always leads us to live a crucified life, conforming us to the death of Christ. In Philippians 3:10 Paul said that He desired to know Christ, the power of His resurrection, and the fellowship of His sufferings, being conformed to His death. The wonderful Spirit works to conform us to the death of Christ.

THE CROSS

The cross of Christ is the negative consummation of the work of Christ (1 Cor. 1:17-18; Gal. 6:12). The cross of Christ has put away sin (Heb. 9:26), has destroyed the devil, Satan (Heb. 2:14; Col. 2:15), has crucified the world and us (Gal. 6:14b; 2:20a), and has crucified our old man (Rom. 6:6). The cross of Christ has also abolished the ordinances of the law (Eph. 2:15; Col. 2:14). The top ordinances among the Jews were those concerning circumcision, keeping the Sabbath, and the holy diet. There are also countless ordinances in the human race. Ordinances are the forms or ways of living and worship. All of our ordinances have to go to the cross. Then we can have a genuine oneness with harmony in Christ for the Body of Christ. In the universe there is such an all-inclusive death that has killed all the separating ordinances among men. But sometimes these separating ordinances may creep into the church life. This is why we need the all-inclusive death of Christ. We have to realize that our destiny is to be crucified, and we must take a crucified way. Whatever we are, has to be crucified.

The cross of Christ is applied to us by the Spirit (Rom. 8:13b). In the Spirit, there is the killing element of the cross. When we live by the Spirit, the Spirit within us will kill all the negative things, such as sin, Satan, the world, me, the old man, and all the differences due to ordinances. We need to apply the cross of Christ to our flesh with the passions and the lusts through the cooperation with the Spirit (Gal. 5:24).

The experience of the cross of Christ issues in the abundance of the Spirit of life. According to Galatians 2:20, the more we experience the cross of Christ, the more Christ lives in us. John 12:24 shows that the Lord's death as a grain of wheat issued in much fruit. When we experience the death of Christ, the issue is the multiplication of life. Furthermore, we boast in the cross of Christ (Gal. 6:14a). The cross was really an abasement, but the Apostle Paul made it his boast.

The Spirit brings us to the cross. If we take the cross, the cross will issue in more of the Spirit. Before Christ went to the cross, the Spirit was always leading Him. This leading Spirit always led Him to the cross. The entire life of Christ was a life led by the Spirit to the cross. Christ lived a crucified life, a life under the cross for thirty-three and a half years. Every day of His life, He was being crucified by the Holy Spirit. Even when He went to the physical cross for six hours, He went there by the eternal Spirit of God and offered Himself to God through this Spirit (Heb. 9:14). Therefore, the Spirit comes first and then the cross. When we were saved, the first thing we received was the Spirit. Then from that time onward, this Spirit leads us to the cross. We have to undergo the process of being crossed out all the time by allowing the Spirit to bring us to the cross, so that the cross can issue in more of the Spirit.

ABOUT THE AUTHOR

Witness Lee was born in 1905 in northern China and raised in a Christian family. At age 19 he was fully captured for Christ and immediately consecrated himself to preach the gospel for the rest of his life. Early in his service, he met Watchman Nee, a renowned preacher, teacher, and writer. Witness Lee labored together with Watchman Nee under his direction. In 1934 Watchman Nee entrusted Witness Lee with the responsibility for his publication operation, called the Shanghai Gospel Bookroom.

Prior to the Communist takeover in 1949, Witness Lee was sent by Watchman Nee and his other co-workers to Taiwan to ensure that the things delivered to them by the Lord would not be lost. Watchman Nee instructed Witness Lee to continue the former's publishing operation abroad as the Taiwan Gospel Bookroom, which has been publicly recognized as the publisher of Watchman Nee's works outside China. Witness Lee's work in Taiwan manifested the Lord's abundant blessing. From a mere 350 believers, newly fled from the mainland, the churches in Taiwan grew to 20,000 in five years.

In 1962 Witness Lee felt led of the Lord to come to the United States, and he began to minister in Los Angeles. During his 35 years of service in the U.S., he ministered in weekly meetings and weekend conferences, delivering several thousand spoken messages. Much of his speaking has since been published as over 400 titles. Many of these have been translated into over fourteen languages. He gave his last public conference in February 1997 at the age of 91.

He leaves behind a prolific presentation of the truth in the Bible. His major work, *Life-study of the Bible,* comprises over 25,000 pages of commentary on every book of the Bible from the perspective of the believers' enjoyment and experience of God's divine life in Christ through the Holy Spirit. Witness Lee was the chief editor of a new translation of the New Testament into Chinese called the Recovery Version and directed the translation of the same into English. The Recovery Version also appears in a number of other languages. He provided an extensive body of footnotes, outlines, and spiritual cross references. A radio broadcast of his messages can be heard on Christian radio stations in the United States. In 1965 Witness Lee founded Living Stream Ministry, a non-profit corporation, located in Anaheim, California, which officially presents his and Watchman Nee's ministry.

Witness Lee's ministry emphasizes the experience of Christ as life and the practical oneness of the believers as the Body of Christ. Stressing the importance of attending to both these matters, he led the churches under his care to grow in Christian life and function. He was unbending in his conviction that God's goal is not narrow sectarianism but the Body of Christ. In time, believers began to meet simply as the church in their localities in response to this conviction. In recent years a number of new churches have been raised up in Russia and in many European countries.